A DEATH
IN BELMONT

ALSO BY SEBASTIAN JUNGER

The Perfect Storm

Fire

SEBASTIAN JUNGER

A DEATH IN BELMONT

W. W. NORTON & COMPANY

NEW YORK • LONDON

Photograph of Albert DeSalvo with police officers in Cambridge, Massachussetts, used by permission of Associated Press.

For information about permission to reproduce selections from this book, write to Permissions, W. W. Norton & Company, Inc., 500 Fifth Avenue, New York, NY 10110

Manufacturing by RR Donnelley, Harrisonburg, VA

Book design by Chris Welch

Production manager: Anna Oler

Library of Congress Cataloging-in-Publication Data

Junger, Sebastian.

A death in Belmont / Sebastian Junger.—1st ed.

p. cm.

Includes bibliographical references.

ISBN-13: 978-0-393-05980-9 (hardcover)

ISBN-10: 0-393-05980-4 (hardcover)

1. Murder—Massachusetts—Belmont—Case studies. 2. Smith, Roy, 1927 or 8– 3. Goldberg, Bessie. 4. De Salvo, Albert Henry, 1931– I. Title.

HV6534.B43J86 2006

364.152'3097444—dc22   2006000488

W. W. Norton & Company, Inc.

500 Fifth Avenue, New York, N.Y. 10110

www.wwnorton.com

W. W. Norton & Company Ltd.

Castle House, 75/76 Wells Street, London W1T 3QT

1 2 3 4 5 6 7 8 9 0

FOR MY MOTHER,
ELLEN SINCLAIR JUNGER

And they said to the Prophet, "How may we stop our ears to the rant of the fool and yet show him charity?"

And he answered, "You show yourselves charity by opening wide your ears to him. The fool in the midst of his babble shall speak truths which the minds of the wise cannot perceive."

—unattributed quote pinned to the office
wall of a Massachusetts appellate lawyer

A NOTE ON QUOTES

If a passage is enclosed in quotation marks in this book, it means that the person was speaking into a tape recorder or before a court stenographer. In some instances I wrote my interviews in notebooks, but that was rare; almost all my interviews were done with a tape recorder. Conversations in this book were obviously not recorded as they happened, so they never take quotation marks. As reproduced in this book, however, they do faithfully represent the recollections of the people involved. In all cases—including in some published texts—I have made grammatical changes for the sake of clarity, as well as minor edits for the sake of brevity.

THE
MURDER

ONE

ONE MORNING IN the fall of 1962, when I was not yet one year old, my mother, Ellen, looked out the window and saw two men in our front yard. One was in his thirties and the other was at least twice that, and they were both dressed in work clothes and seemed very interested in the place where we lived. My mother picked me up and walked outside to see what they wanted.

They turned out to be carpenters who had stopped to look at our house because one of them—the older man—had built it. He said his name was Floyd Wiggins and that twenty years earlier he'd built our house in sections up in Maine and then brought them down by truck. He said he assembled it on-site in a single day. We lived in a placid little suburb of Boston called Belmont, and my parents had always thought that our house looked a little out of place. It had an offset salt-box roof and blue clapboard siding and stingy little sash windows that were good for conserving heat. Now it made sense: The house had been built by an old Maine carpenter who must have designed it after the farmhouses he saw all around him.

Wiggins now lived outside Boston and worked for the younger man, who introduced himself as Russ Blomerth. He had a painting job around the corner, Blomerth said, and that was why they were in the neighborhood. My mother said that the house was wonderful but too small and that she and my father were taking bids from contractors to build a studio addition out back. She was an artist, she explained, and the studio would allow her to paint and give drawing classes at home while keeping an eye on me. Would they be interested in the job? Blomerth said that he would be, so my mother put me in his arms and ran inside to get a copy of the architectural plans.

Blomerth's bid was the low one, as it turned out, and within a few weeks he, Wiggins, and a younger man named Al were in the backyard laying the foundation for my mother's studio. Some days all three men showed up, some days it was Blomerth and Wiggins, some days it was just Al. Around eight o'clock in the morning my mother would hear the bulkhead door slam, and then she'd hear footsteps in the basement as Al got his tools, and then a few minutes later she'd watch him cross the backyard to start work. Al never went into the main part of the house, but sometimes my mother would bring a sandwich out to the studio and keep him company while he ate lunch. Al talked a lot about his children and his German wife. Al had served with the American forces in postwar Germany and been the middleweight champion of the American army in Europe. Al was polite and deferential to my mother and worked hard without saying much. Al had dark hair and a powerful build and a prominent beak of a nose and was not, my mother says, an unhandsome man.

My mother was born in Canton, Ohio, the year of the stock market crash to a nightclub and amusement park owner named Carl

Sinclair and his wife, Marjorie. Canton was a conservative little city that could be stifling to a woman who wanted more than a husband and children—which, as it turned out, my mother did. She wanted to be an artist. At eighteen she moved to Boston, went to art school, and then rented a studio and started to paint. Her parents looked on with alarm. Young women of her generation did not pass up marriage for art, and that was exactly what my mother seemed to be doing. A few years went by and she hadn't married, and a decade went by and she still hadn't married, and by the time she met my father, Miguel, in the bar of the Ritz Hotel her parents had all but given up.

When my mother finally got married at age twenty-nine it was welcome news, but my father could not have been exactly what her parents had envisioned. The son of a Russian-born journalist who wrote in French, and a beautiful Austrian socialite, he had come to the United States during the war to escape the Nazis and study physics at Harvard. He spoke five languages, he could recite the names of most of the Roman emperors, and he had no idea how the game of baseball was played. He also had made it to age thirty-seven without getting married, which alarmed any number of my mother's female friends. Against their advice she eloped with him to San Francisco, and they were married by a judge at the city hall. A year later my mother got pregnant with me, and they bought a house in a pretty little suburb called Belmont.

The studio they built, when it was finally finished, had a high cement foundation set into a slight hill and end walls of fir planks with a steep-pitched shingle roof that came down almost to the ground. There was a Plexiglas skylight at the roof peak that poured light onto the tile floors, and there was a raised flagstone landing that my mother populated with large plants. The job was completed in the spring of 1963; by then Blomerth and Wiggins had moved on to other work, and Al was left by himself to finish up the last details and paint the trim. On one of those last days of the job, my mother dropped me off at my baby-sitter's and went into town to do some errands and then picked me up at the end of the day. We weren't home twenty minutes when the phone rang. It was the baby-sitter, an Irishwoman I knew as Ani, and she was in a panic. Lock up the house, Ani told my mother. The Boston Strangler just killed someone in Belmont.

The victim's name was Bessie Goldberg, and she had been found by her husband raped and strangled in their home on Scott Road. Several days earlier, a sixty-eight-year-old woman named Mary Brown had been raped and bludgeoned to death in the small town of Lawrence, north of Boston. They were the eighth and ninth sex murders in the Boston area in almost a year, and the city was in a state of terror. My mother rushed out to the studio where Al was painting on a ladder and told him the news. It's so scary, my mother remembers telling him. I mean, here he is in Belmont, for God's sake! Al shook his head and said how terrible it was, and he and my mother talked about it for a while, and eventually she went back into the house to start dinner.

My mother didn't see Al again until the next day. He showed up with Blomerth and Wiggins because the job was almost done and they had to start packing their tools and cleaning up the site. Blomerth had brought a camera for the occasion, and he arranged us all inside the studio and took a photograph. I'm looking straight at Blomerth—no doubt because he said something to get my attention—and my mother, seated on a maplewood bench, is looking down at me, her firstborn child, rather than up at the camera. She is thirty-four years old, and her dark brown hair is pinned high on her head and she wears a paisley shirt with the sleeves neatly rolled up and she appears primarily interested in the baby on her lap. Behind my mother and off her right shoulder is old Mister Wiggins standing politely in a sweater-vest with his hands clasped behind his back and a claw hammer jammed headfirst into his front pocket. His shirt is buttoned right up to his chin, and he looks like he's at least seventy-five years old. Standing next to Wiggins and directly behind my mother is Al.

Al and I are the only people looking directly at the camera, and whereas I have an infant's expression of puzzled amazement, Al wears an odd smirk. His dark hair is greased up in a pompadour, and he is clean-shaven but unmistakably rough looking, and he has placed across his stomach one enormous, outspread hand. The hand is visible only because my mother is leaning forward to look at me. The hand is at the exact center of the photograph, as if it were the true subject around which the rest of us have been arranged.

TWO

ICE WASN'T UNTIL Israel Goldberg started putting the food away in the kitchen that he realized something was wrong. His wife, Bessie, had asked him to pick up frozen vegetables and cheese on his way home from work, but when he pushed open the front door and called out her name, all he heard was the radio. That was odd; Bessie had hired a cleaning man to help get the house ready for a dinner party that night, and Israel had expected to find them both at work when he arrived home. Instead, the house was deserted and there wasn't even a note. Bess! he shouted from the kitchen, but still no one answered, and that was when his puzzlement turned to fear. He dropped his overcoat on the floor and ran upstairs, calling his wife's name as he went. He checked thir bedroom. He checked their closets. He checked the spare bedroom. He checked their daughter's old bedroom: no one.

Outside, Israel could hear the shouts of children playing kickball on the street; a boy named Dougie Dreyer was single-handedly scoring run after run against an assemblage of neighborhood girls.

John F. Kennedy was president, America was not yet at war, and Belmont, Massachusetts, where he and his wife had moved ten years earlier, was arguably the epitome of all that was safe and peaceful in the world. There were no bars or liquor stores in Belmont. There were no poor people in Belmont. There were no homeless people in Belmont. There were no dangerous parts of Belmont, or poor parts of Belmont, or even ugly parts of Belmont. There had never been a murder in Belmont. It was—until the moment Israel Goldberg went back downstairs and finally glanced into the living room—the ideal place to live.

The first thing he noticed was his wife's feet, which protruded from behind the corner of the wall. Israel stepped into the living room to investigate. A standing lamp had been knocked over, and its pedestal was now propped on the arm of the divan. Between the lampshade and the knocked-over lamp lay the immobile body of his wife.

Bessie Goldberg was on her back with her skirt and apron pulled up and her legs exposed. One of her stockings had been wound around her neck, and her eyes were open, and there was a little bit of blood on her lip. The first thought that went through Israel Goldberg's mind was that he'd never seen his wife wearing a scarf before. An instant later he realized that her head was at the wrong angle, that her face looked puffy and that she wasn't breathing. According to the children on the street, Israel Goldberg was inside less than a couple of minutes before he screamed and ran back out and demanded to know if they had seen anyone leave the house. They hadn't, though they would later remember a black man passing them on the sidewalk as they walked home from school. A black man was not a common sight in Belmont in 1963, and virtually every good citizen who had seen him walking down Pleasant Street that afternoon remembered him.

In hindsight—Belmont now forever marred by its first murder—some witnesses agreed that the black man might have looked like he was in a hurry. He had glanced back several times. He had walked fast, hands in his coat pockets, and had almost walked into some bushes as he passed Dougie Dreyer and two neighborhood girls on their way home from school. A sub-shop owner named Louis Pizzuto caught sight of him from behind his restaurant counter and was sufficiently curious to step around to the doorway to watch him pass. The black man had stopped in at the Pleasant Street Pharmacy across the street and then reemerged a few minutes later with a pack of cigarettes. The teenage boy who worked at the pharmacy said that he had bought a pack of Pall Malls for twenty-eight cents but had not seemed nervous. A middle-aged woman said that he hadn't seemed nervous but that the skin of his face was "pocky." Sometime later Louis Pizzuto walked into the pharmacy to make sure everything was okay. So what did the big darkie want?—or something much like that—he asked the boy behind the counter.

Not much, it seemed, except the cigarettes. The black man was tall and thin and wore brown checked pants and a black overcoat. Some remembered him wearing a dark hat and sunglasses, and some remembered that he had a moustache and sideburns. Soon it would be known that he crossed the street to the bus stop and boarded the first bus that came, which, unfortunately, was going in the wrong direction. Instead of getting off, he stayed on it to Park Circle, smoked a cigarette with the bus driver during the five-minute layover and then continued back toward Cambridge. He stepped off the bus in Harvard Square at nineteen minutes to four and walked past Out-of-Town News to the closest bar he could find. He would have been sitting at the bar counter ordering a ten-cent beer just as Israel Goldberg opened the door of his strangely quiet home. He would have been in a taxicab heading toward a friend's apartment in Central Square when police cruisers began converging on Scott Road. And he would have been walking around Central Square looking for his girlfriend—who had left him several days earlier—when Leah Goldberg, Bessie and Israel's twenty-four-year-old daughter, arrived at the murder scene and was led by a police officer to her stunned and grief-struck father.

Leah chose not to look at her mother's body; the last time she'd seen her mother was at dinner the night before, and she wanted to keep it that way. She did cast around the house, though, and spotted on the kitchen counter a piece of paper that the police officers had missed. It was from the Massachusetts Employment Security Office on Huntington Avenue in Boston, and it had a name written on it. Shortly after that discovery the phone rang, and a woman named Mrs. Martin asked for Israel Goldberg. Mrs. Martin said she was calling from the Massachusetts Division of Employment Security and just wanted to know how the new cleaning man had worked out.

He murdered my wife, that's how he worked out! Israel Goldberg screamed into the phone.

The name on the employment stub was Roy Smith. Smith was originally from Oxford, Mississippi, but his records at Employment Security had him living at 441 Blue Hill Avenue in Roxbury. That wasn't true; he really lived with his girlfriend at 175 Northampton Street in Boston. The landlady, however, told the police that Smith's girlfriend had moved out four or five days earlier. Two plainclothes officers stayed on Northampton Street while word went out to the Cambridge police station that Smith might be in the area looking for his girlfriend. At 11:13 p.m. the police issued a bulletin, accompanied by Roy Smith's mug shots and fingerprint data from a previous arrest, announcing that he was wanted for murder in the town of Belmont. Bessie Goldberg was the ninth Boston-area woman to be raped and strangled in less than a year, and many of the victims had been elderly. If Roy Smith had indeed killed Bessie Goldberg—and by now the authorities knew that his criminal history included grand larceny, assault with a dangerous weapon, and public drunkenness—they had their first break in a series of murders that had virtually paralyzed the city of Boston.

The public called the killer the "Boston Strangler," and a special investigatory unit—the "Strangler Bureau"—had been convened to track him down. They had screened 2,500 sex offenders and brought in 300 of them for close questioning. They had interviewed 5,000 people connected to the victims and combed through half a million fingerprint files. It was the most thorough investigation in Massachusetts history, and their spectacular lack of success was leading the public to attribute nearly supernatural qualities to the killer: He was inhumanly strong; he could break into any apartment, no matter how well-locked; he could kill in minutes and leave no trace at all. Women bought guard dogs. They only went out in pairs. They placed cans in darkened hallways as a sort of early-warning system. One particularly high-strung woman heard someone in her apartment and leaped to her death from her third-floor window rather than face whatever it was. Virtually every month there was another sick, brutal murder in Boston, and the fifty-man tactical police unit—specially trained in karate and quick-draw shooting—was helpless to stop them.

"What I remember about Roy Smith," says Mike Giacoppo, the Cambridge police officer who arrested him, "is that they had a murder warrant out for him, and that they said it was possible he'd be in Cambridge or in Somerville. I used to work for a power and light company, and they have a database that's unreal. So I went to the power and light company at night and looked up names. Every time I found an R. Smith moved in or moved out, I'd find a D. Hunt, which was Dorothy Hunt. They would move out without paying their bills, you know; they'd shut 'em off. I finally located her at 93 Brookline Street in Cambridge. And so I went up to the captain, and I says, 'I got a hunch.'"

Giacoppo's captain wouldn't let him do a stakeout on the clock because he was just a rookie, so Giacoppo waited until his shift was over to drive over to 93 Brookline Street. He was in civilian clothes, and he had another rookie friend with him named Billy Coughlin. The house was a triple-decker on a street that ran north–south from the Charles River to the Irish bars and shoe stores of Central Square—a working-class part of Cambridge known as "the Coast." Giacoppo parked across from 93 Brookline Street and got out of the car and started for a variety store where he planned to ask if anyone knew Dorothy Hunt. Halfway there he saw a little black girl sitting on the stoop, and he stopped in front of her and bent down and asked her instead. The girl said that that was her mother. Is Roy up there? Giacoppo asked. The girl said yes.

Giacoppo and Coughlin had no radio and no backup and were possibly about to arrest the most prolific killer in Boston history. If they drove back to the police station to get help, Smith might escape. If they tried to go in and arrest him, they might find themselves in way over their heads. Giacoppo walked across the street to the variety store to use the telephone, but the owner said he didn't have one. There was only one thing left to do: He told Coughlin to go up the front stairs of the building and he pulled his gun and went up the back stairs. When he got to the top landing he pounded on the door until a black man named Ronald Walcott finally let him in.

Smith was frozen in an armchair, and Coughlin was pointing his service revolver at his head and screaming that he would shoot him if he moved. Dorothy Hunt and her other young daughter looked on in shock. Smith asked what he was being arrested for, and Coughlin told him that it was suspicion of murder. Smith didn't say anything in response. "He was in a state of shock," says Giacoppo. "How would you be if you had a gun to your head? We held a gun to his head all the way. We never handcuffed him—we didn't even have handcuffs with us! It was sort of a comedy of errors, it was a riot, we did everything wrong."

They took Smith down the back staircase and then out onto the street, revolvers still pointing at his head. Smith never said a word. One of the cops flagged down a car, and all three men squeezed into the back seat, and Giacoppo yelled at the terrified driver to take them to the police station. The station was just around the corner, and minutes later Smith found himself seated in a chair getting booked by a detective named Leo Davenport. A photograph that appeared on the front page of the *Boston Herald* shows Davenport in a suit and tie working away on a manual typewriter while Coughlin and Giacoppo and another police officer look on from behind. Smith is seated in a chair with one hand shackled to the armrest and the other cocked up in the air with a cigarette between his first and second fingers. His legs are crossed, and he is looking down at his knees. The accompanying article describes him as a "lean, moustached drifter" who wore a striped sports shirt and shabby brown trousers and ignored the crowd that had gathered around him except to avert his face from the news cameras.

The way Bessie Goldberg died was considered a classic "Boston Strangling," so Smith's arrest prompted many local reporters to announce that the Strangler had finally been caught. The few reporters who held back on that announcement resorted to a theme of random violence in the suburbs that was almost as compelling. Until now all the stranglings had occurred in apartment buildings in downtown Boston or in working-class towns north of the city. Bessie Goldberg was the first woman to be killed in a one-family home in an affluent neighborhood, and if a murderer could strike there, he could strike anywhere. "This is Belmont, these things just don't happen here!" one of Bessie's neighbors told the *Boston Herald*. Another reporter described the Goldberg house as a "rambling ten-room colonial . . . on a street of similarly expensive homes." In fact it was a modest brick-and-clapboard on a street that virtually overlooked a highway. It was also imagined by the press that Bessie Goldberg had put up a "terrific struggle" for her life, though there was little evidence of that. She had, in fact, died with her glasses on. The details of sexual assault, of course, were respectfully muted.

Whether or not Smith was the Boston Strangler, the case against him for the Goldberg murder was devastating. By his own admission he had been at the Goldberg house most of the afternoon and had left around three o'clock, a fact confirmed by numerous people in the neighborhood. Israel Goldberg had arrived home at ten minutes to four—again confirmed by numerous people—and no one had spotted anyone else going into or out of the Goldberg house during the intervening fifty minutes. The house was in disarray, as if Smith had not finished cleaning, and fifteen dollars that Israel had left on Bessie's nightstand was missing. As far as the police were concerned, Smith had committed the murder because, realistically, no one else could have. All that remained was for Smith to confess, which—considering the evidence against him—seemed almost inevitable. If Smith confessed to second-degree murder and served his time peacefully, he could expect to be out in fifteen years or so. For a habitual criminal accused of murder in a city terrorized by a serial killer, it wasn't a bad deal.

IT HAS BEEN forty years since her mother's murder, and Leah Goldberg—now older than her mother was when she died—still cannot talk about it without getting angry. She is a small, intense woman who speaks her mind sharply and unapologetically, her voice occasionally diving into an outraged whisper that even the person she is speaking to cannot understand. She was living in Cambridge and teaching fifth graders at the Roberts School at the time of the murder; she first heard something was wrong when the operator broke into a phone conversation and said that she had an emergency call for a Leah Goldberg. It was her father. He told her that her mother was sick and to come home as quickly as possible.

Leah could tell from her father's voice that the news was really far worse. She dropped the phone, and she and one of her roommates dashed out to her car and drove down Concord Avenue to Belmont Center and then turned up Pleasant Street to her old neighborhood. There was a police cruiser and an ambulance in front of her house, and neighborhood children watching from the street. Leah ran up to the front door and caught a glimpse of her father through the living room window. He saw her as well and just raised his arms in grief.

Leah's memories of the next few hours are jumbled. She answered a lot of questions from the police but was in such a state of shock that the exchanges were utterly calm. The police sent her to a neighbor's house to recover, but later she could not remember whether her father had come with her or not. She had trouble making sense of the fact that she had seen her mother just the previous evening; everything that followed seemed like an insane dream that inevitably had to end. It was not a dream, and it was not going to end. Not only had her mother's life been truncated, but in some ways her father's life had as well. He was sixty-eight years old and had been married to Bessie for almost half of that. He was the one who had discovered the body. He was the one who had rushed over to help his wife and then realized that she was dead. Every morning for the rest of his life he would have to greet that image in his mind and then fence it out and somehow keep it out of his thoughts for the rest of the day until it was time to go to sleep again. He would have to do that for another twenty-six years. It was worse than any sentence Smith could get from a judge.

The unsavory details about Smith helped make sense of the crime but also raised other agonizing issues. Mrs. Martin at the Division of Employment Security thought she might have smelled alcohol on his breath. So why did she send him on the job? It was known that Smith had an extensive criminal record. How could Mrs. Martin have failed to warn Leah's mother that an ex-con was coming to clean her house? Police investigators also thought that Smith might be a drug addict or have an extremely low IQ. Is that why he would commit a murder that he was virtually certain to get caught for? The aspects of Smith's personality that could explain his impulsive murder inevitably made the crime seem senseless and avoidable.

It was possible, Leah Goldberg realized, that her mother had died simply because Roy Smith had wanted to get high. It seemed hard to believe, but why else would someone kill another person for the fifteen dollars on their nightstand?

THREE

R OY SMITH WAS born in Oxford, Mississippi, on the Fourth of July in either 1927 or 1928; court documents list one year or the other, and the murder indictment lists both, followed by a question mark. Presumably even Smith himself wasn't sure. Smith stood five feet eleven, was rail thin and had a two-inch scar over his left eye and another deep scar on his left hand from a broken milk bottle. He told police that he never regained full use of the hand. A booking photo taken after his arrest shows a thin, resigned-looking man gazing carefully down from the camera, as if he wanted to avoid anything that might be mistaken for defiance. His brows angled inward and downward in a strange permanent frown. His eyes were bloodshot and his nose looked broken toward the right, as if someone had punched him that way, and he had a fine, narrow face that women must have noticed.

Both of Smith's parents worked at the University of Mississippi in Oxford, known as Ole Miss. His father, Andrew, was a janitor and an itinerant minister, and his mother, Mollie, was a cafeteria worker at the gymnasium. Mollie worked under a legendary baseball coach named Tad Smith, a man of such local stature that people were given to naming their children after him. Southerners of that generation, both black and white, occasionally named their children after people or causes they admired; first names like "State's Rights" or "Ex-Senator Webb" were not unheard of in Mississippi when Roy was growing up. Mollie and Andrew named Roy's younger brother "Coach," after Tad Smith. They pronounced it *Co-ach*, though, with two syllables and both vowels enunciated.

Coach was three or four years younger than Roy. In addition Roy had an older brother named Lerone, an older half brother named Tommy Hudson—born to fourteen-year-old Mollie by another man—two younger brothers, and three sisters. Most of the family was described in court papers as "loyal," which possibly meant that they believed Roy was innocent. A written report by a Mississippi probation officer, requested by the Massachusetts courts, stated that "The Smiths all have a good reputation in and around Oxford, this was attested to by Sheriff Joe Ford. It seems this is the first trouble any of the Smith children have been into."

The family lived on South Sixteenth street, in a wood-frame house that they owned. The area was farmland back then—before the highway truncated South Sixteenth, before an urban renewal project converted sharecropper shacks to brick ranch-styles, before the city limits expanded and prohibited the keeping of livestock and poultry. Back then many people in Oxford—even successful business owners—kept chickens and a milk cow and tended a vegetable garden. As late as the 1960s, black farmers sold vegetables off mule carts on the town square and took their cotton to the gin in lumbering, overloaded wagons. Andrew, the father, preached on weekends at the invitation of local ministers, at the New Hope Baptist Church and the Second Baptist Church and the Clear Creek Church. He grew up illiterate but learned to read the Bible with the help of his wife. He was known for his devotion to his wife and to God and hard work, and he was also known for his fondness for women. Weeknights he would sit in an armchair and watch television while reading the Bible, and weekends he would preach and chew tobacco and chat up the women in the congregation.

The family property was adjacent to a large tract called Brown's Farm, and Roy grew up picking cotton for Mr. Ross Brown. Picking cotton for someone else was an excellent way to die young, exhausted, and poor. When Roy's parents were growing up in Oxford, 80 percent of the local black population had fallen into sharecropping, and things hadn't improved much by the time Roy was old enough to start working. Under the sharecropping system the landowner provided the land and tools and tenant farmers did the work; profits were split down the middle. Poor whites fell into sharecropping as well as blacks. In theory the sharecropping arrangement should have made the landowner and sharecropper equal partners in the enterprise of growing crops; in reality the system couldn't have been better designed to encourage exploitation.

Because the landowners were in charge of selling the crops, they could report almost any profit they wanted. They could also deduct the cost of tools, seed, and household items off the top, all of which the sharecroppers had bought from the landowner at inflated prices and obscene interest rates. At the end of the year many sharecroppers discovered that their profits barely covered their debts, and they got nothing for all their work. The sharecropping system was so good at keeping cash out of the hands of tenant farmers that as late as the 1950s in Mississippi, there were people who had never seen a dollar bill.

The Smith family had not been sucked into the sharecropping trap, but the work that Roy did at Ross Brown's was nevertheless a backbreaking business. "The Mississippi Delta will kill a dog in five years, a mule in ten, and a man in twenty," the saying went. The hardest work was in September, when the cotton bolls burst open and turned the land as white as if it had snowed. Jails were emptied, schools were closed, and most of the black population of Oxford took to the fields with six-foot picking bags over their shoulders. A ragged line of pickers moving across a field looked like hunchbacks in a slow-motion race. A full sack weighed between 100 and 150 pounds, depending on its size, and a man could fill three bags in a day if he worked hard. The job required both an infuriating dexterity to pick the cotton lint out of the razor-sharp bolls, and a bullish strength to drag the bag across the fields. As a result of this odd pairing of skills, the strongest people were not necessarily the fastest; men picked cotton, women picked cotton, children as young as ten picked cotton, and occasionally a woman came along who could outpick the men.

Because they lived in town, Andrew and Mollie's children had options that farm kids did not. Roy's brother Coach got a job working at Belk Motors in Oxford; his brother Lerone made his living installing air conditioners in Memphis; and James became a carpenter. Roy was the only brother who didn't finish high school, quitting at age fourteen to start working at a chain grocery store called the Jitney Jungle. The Jitney, on the north side of the square, was an Oxford institution that eventually moved a couple of blocks to North Lamar before fading out completely. The store sold canned pork brain and hog testicles and ears and jowls, and packages simply labeled "meat." People got rides out of town in front of the Jitney and picked up day work in front of the Jitney and met their girlfriends in front of the Jitney. Much of Oxford life happened in front of the Jitney, and Roy, as a teenager, would have been exposed to the best and worst of it.

Facing a life in Ross Brown's fields or the in aisles of the Jitney, Roy decided in July 1945 to join the U.S. Marine Corps. The military was a popular option for black men in the Deep South in the 1940s; in addition to a regular paycheck and technical training, they were also able to escape the oppressive racism of their hometowns. The military, if not entirely color blind, was at least crudely egalitarian. Roy served two years in the South Pacific and was honorably discharged in Pensacola, Florida, in August 1947. He probably drifted west with whatever was left of his service pay, maybe visiting relatives in Memphis or Chicago. Many black servicemen found returning home an agonizing prospect. Whereas in the military, black units had served side by side with white units and had been judged more or less on their own merits, these men were now returning to the segregated lunch counters and humiliating work conditions of the Deep South. When Roy Smith was growing up, black men were still getting beaten up for not stepping off the sidewalk and tipping their hats when a white lady passed. For a young black man who had fought—and maybe had even been wounded—in World War II, returning to an environment like that must have been psychologically devastating.

Roy Smith first entered the legal system on February 8, 1949, when he was arrested with his older brother, Lerone, and another man, named Butch Roberson, for public drinking. The two Smith brothers pleaded guilty to being drunk and "using profane language in the presence of two or more persons" and were fined twenty dollars and released. Roberson, who owned a whiskey still and had undoubtedly supplied the booze that night, was fined a hundred dollars and also released. The fine was recorded to have been paid by a man named "JWT Falkner," a well-known lawyer in Oxford who was also an uncle of the famous writer William Faulkner. (William had already taken to spelling his family name differently.) John Wesley Thompson Falkner II often represented indigent black men in court—not out of any kind of idealism but because there was steady work in it. This was not the last time he would have to deal with the Smith family.

Of all the Smith sons, Lerone was the one with the wild streak, with the knack for inviting the attention of the law. Lerone grew up stealing chickens from people's backyards and selling them in town. Lerone was in trouble with the law so continually that he would take off running at the sight of a policeman whether he'd done anything wrong or not. There were times when Lerone had to sleep under other peoples' houses to avoid being arrested. When Lerone was older he got a shack out in the country where he bootlegged, raised hogs, worked on old tractors, and had parties. The place was a half hour drive down a dirt road from the nearest highway, and people would show up at all hours to drink, gamble, and carry on in ways that they couldn't in town.

It was with Lerone, of course, that Roy had his first very serious encounter with Sheriff Boyce Bratton.

THE LAFAYETTE COUNTY Courthouse dominates Oxford from the center of the town square. It is a whitewashed two-story building with high arched windows and four fluted columns on a second-floor veranda that looks out over huge, graceful water oaks. A four-faced clock on the roof peak theoretically gave the time to every person in town, though it was often broken. A granite statue

of a Confederate soldier on the south side of the building com-
memorates the young men who "gave their lives in a just and holy
cause." It is worth noting that one out of three men in Mississippi's
armed forces died for that cause, and that one-fifth of the state
budget went to fitting the survivors with artificial limbs. In Oxford
war fever ran so high that virtually the entire student body of the
University of Mississippi enlisted en masse, closing the school.
Their regiment, called the University Grays, suffered a 100 percent
casualty rate during the infamous Pickett's charge at the battle of
Gettysburg; every single man in the regiment was either killed,
wounded, or captured before they reached the top of Seminary
Ridge. Inside the double oak doors of the courthouse, through the
clerk's office on the right, in a small windowless room in the back,
rows of leatherbound docket books lean haphazardly on shelves.

The books are two feet high and broken down at the spine and
embossed with gold lettering. In the volume that includes 1949, on
page 312, under the date March 17, Roy Smith's name is entered
with the charge of burglary and a bail of one thousand dollars. It
had been hardly a month since Roy's last encounter with the law,
and this time he was with Lerone and his half brother, Tommy
Hudson. Tommy and Lerone supposedly didn't get along very well,
but they got along well enough to get arrested together.

Lerone and Tommy were arrested first, and Roy was picked up
the following day. They were arrested by Sheriff Bratton, who may
have simply gone to Andy Smith's place on South Sixteenth and told
him that he wanted the boys to turn themselves in. Bratton stood
only five feet eight but was so feared that he didn't even bother to
wear a gun. When he had to arrest someone, he simply showed up
at their home and told them they were coming downtown; invariably they complied. The jail was a two-story brick building on the

east side of the square, with a kitchen on the first floor where the jailer's wife cooked for the inmates, and a single cell on the second floor where the inmates slept. The cell was secured by a massive door hewed from a single slab of oak that was hung on iron hinges and locked by an iron bar padlocked through two iron hasps. It still had bullet holes in it from an earlier lynching. A single window, crudely barred, gave the inmates a view of the streets in which they had just committed their crimes. "The dark limber hands would lie in the grimed interstices," William Faulkner wrote in 1948 about the Oxford jailhouse window, "while the mellow untroubled repentless voices would shout down to the women in the aprons of cooks or nurses and the girls in their flash cheap clothes from the mail order houses or the other young men who had not been caught yet or had been caught and freed yesterday, gathered along the street."

Roy and Tommy and Lerone had committed the sin of stealing cotton. Tommy owned an old Packard, and the three brothers had driven it out to a farm owned by a big planter named Guy McCarty and sent Roy into the "cotton house," where the raw cotton was stored, to drag out four or five bags. Cotton was going for fifty or sixty cents a pound back then—the war had caused cotton prices to skyrocket—and a trunk full of cotton would have been worth hundreds of dollars. It would have been an enormous amount of money for them, even split three ways—but it also put them way over the fifty-dollar limit for grand larceny. They apparently made it off the McCarty place without getting caught but immediately ran into problems back in town. Roy's old boss, Ross Brown, had a cotton gin behind the post office, and Lerone and Tommy drove the cotton there to try to sell it. They must have been asked where the cotton came from almost as soon as they drove onto the scales.

"They probably tried to pass themselves off as sharecroppers," says John Bounds, an Oxford insurance agent who knew the Smith family very well. "Sharecroppers could bring cotton in, but most of the time it would be the farmer. They would have gotten all kinds of questions. 'Where is your land?' 'Which place do you share on?' If you don't have a cotton allotment from the government you can't sell cotton, you can't grow cotton. And the buyer would know every farmer in the county. It wouldn't have taken long for them to ask someone whether Tommy and Lerone were sharecropping for them that year."

Andy raised the thousand-dollar bond to get Roy released, and Roy made an appointment with JWT Falkner to represent him in court. The office was above a barbershop on the town square and was rigged with a water hose to disperse loiterers from the front steps. When Roy walked in he would have found himself standing in front of a simple wood desk with tooled hardwood legs on iron casters. JWT faced him across the desk in a straight-backed slatted swivel chair that was also on casters. The office had old hardwood floors and dented steel filing cabinets and a stamped tin ceiling with magnesium lights and two floor-to-ceiling windows that filtered the daylight through cheap louvered blinds. Falkner probably told Roy that his not-guilty plea didn't have a chance in hell and that the most he, Falkner, could do for him was to minimize his prison time. By prison he would have meant Parchman Farm, a notorious state-run plantation a hundred miles west in the Mississippi Delta. That service would have cost Roy about five hundred dollars, which would have been money well spent. Parchman Farm operated at a profit, in part because it was known for—quite literally—working its inmates to death.

It took almost a year for Roy's case to be heard by Judge Taylor McElroy. An article in the *Oxford Eagle* on March 23, 1950, com-mented that justice had been served at the circuit court that week despite the fact that not a single jury had been convened and not a single witness had been put on the stand. "Just about every defendant pled guilty without a trial," the newspaper gloated, "and are now at Parchman serving their sentence." Twenty-three men—ranging from James Lester, who got eighteen months for operating a whiskey still, to Eugene Chatham, who got natural life for killing his wife on the streets of Oxford—decided not to annoy Judge McElroy by insisting on a trial. Guilty pleas were common in Mississippi courts, by innocent and guilty alike, but clearing an entire slate was remarkable even by the standards of the time. "Roy Smith, colored," the *Eagle* noted in the very last court entry, identifying his race, as was customary. "Burglary, six months."

Roy was now an inmate of the Mississippi State Penitentiary at Parchman Farm.

FOUR

THE BELMONT POLICE had never investigated a murder before—their notes were typed on forms that read "Traffic Bureau Report" at the top—so three additional detectives were sent by the state police. They arrived within an hour of the discovery of Bessie Goldberg's body and immediately began assembling evidence that Roy Smith had committed the crime. Unlike most murders involving strangers, the fact that Smith had been at the Goldbergs' that day wasn't enough to convict him; Smith was supposed to have been there. The very thing that made him a suspect also explained his presence adequately. The detectives needed either a plausible motive for Smith to kill, or they needed physical evidence linking him to the dead body.

At ten-thirty that night—after the murder scene had been photographed, dusted for fingerprints, and sketched and Bessie Goldberg's body had been removed for autopsy—a Belmont police officer named Alfred King interviewed the stricken Israel Goldberg. With King were state police lieutenant John Cahalane and Sgt. Leo

McNulty. Israel Goldberg, of course, was both a witness and—theoretically, anyway—a suspect, though it must have been clear to all of the detectives that this frail sixty-eight-year-old man could not possibly have murdered his wife in the two-minute period between his entering the house and rushing back outside in a panic. Goldberg stated that their regular cleaning man could not come that day, so his wife had called the Massachusetts Employment Security office, and they had sent Roy Smith over. Israel said he had left a ten-dollar bill and five singles with his wife to pay for the work, but none of that money had been found in the house, and neither had the little snap purse that Bessie would have kept it in. The most that Bessie would have paid Smith was six dollars for the work that he had done, plus a little more for bus fare. That meant that eight dollars or so—and a purse—were unaccounted for. If the police could place the purse in Smith's hands, or somehow show that he had more money than he should, a senseless crime would have an obvious logic that any jury could understand. Roy Smith had killed someone for eight dollars and change.

Over the next several days police officers scoured local sewers and street gutters for the missing purse. They checked the Goldberg house as well as the garage of the house next door. They tracked down everyone who lived or worked in the immediate area and took statements from them, and as word of the murder spread, they started to receive calls at the police station from people who thought they could "shed some light" on the matter. Mrs. Lillian Cutliffe, who worked at the Laundromat on Pleasant Street, stated that "she saw a negro walk in front of the shop between 11:30 and 12:00 noon, wearing glasses." Smith also caught the eye of Louis Pizzuto, who owned Gigi's Sub Shop, around 2:30 and 3:00 p.m. "The colored man was in his mid-twenties," Pizzuto told the police, "and wearing a long dark coat that hung below his knees . . . and walked continually looking back." Smith had his hands in his coat pockets, so Pizzuto couldn't tell if he was carrying anything.

Unfortunately no one in the pharmacy saw Smith carrying a purse either, though Smith had bought a pack of Pall Malls for twenty-eight cents. The bus driver who picked Smith up didn't see him carrying a coin purse, and neither did the neighborhood children who passed him on their way home. The children all agreed that he had looked as if he was in a hurry, but their estimates varied on what time it had been. The later Smith left the house, the less time there would be for someone else plausibly to have committed the murder; a time of 3:30 would pretty much nail his case shut. Unfortunately for the police, adult witnesses placed the time around three o'clock, which left a substantial gap—fifty minutes— during which someone else could have killed Bessie Goldberg. It was unlikely, but it was possible, and any good defense attorney could turn a case upside down with the merely possible.

Meanwhile investigators were not getting much help from the body. State police detectives stated in their report that Bessie Goldberg was found on her back in the living room near a divan with a stocking wrapped tightly, but unknotted, around her neck. Her right arm was flung out straight from the shoulder, and her left arm lay across her chest in the same direction. She was fully clothed but for her left shoe, which was lying next to her, and for her left stocking, which was around her neck. Her blouse was pulled halfway open, apparently popping off a button that landed on the divan next to where she lay. Her skirt and underclothes were pulled up in the front, and, as the report put it delicately, "the central portion of her white pants appeared to have been torn out of them completely, exposing her person." Her face was the plum blue of death by strangulation, and there was a spot of blood on the right corner of her mouth. She was still wearing her eyeglasses.

An autopsy was performed several hours later by Dr. Edwin Hill of the Harvard School of Legal Medicine, with Middlesex County medical examiner David Dow looking on. Hill concluded that Bessie Goldberg "came to her death as a result of asphyxia by ligature." Not only was her neck deeply furrowed by the stocking that had strangled her, but her skin and eyelids were covered with numerous pinpoint hemorrhages called petechiae, which are nearly always present in stranglings. Blood cannot drain from the head because of the pressure applied to the neck arteries, so the delicate capillaries near the surface of the tissue eventually burst. Dr. Hill, however, could not find any outward signs of injury to Bessie Goldberg's body. This was mildly unusual but not unheard of. According to a Swedish study, roughly half of strangulation victims have visible wounds on them, mostly bruises and fingernail imprints in the throat. Presumably the weaker—or older—the victim, the less force is necessary to kill them and the fewer injuries they have.

What was odd, though, was the complete lack of injury to Roy Smith. When he was picked up by the Cambridge police, Smith had a small amount of old blood on his pants but no wounds on either of his hands. According to the Swedish study, this is almost unheard of. The study focused on fourteen attacks on adults in which the victim was neither drunk, retarded, nor otherwise incapacitated, and in only one case out of fourteen did the victim fail to wound the attacker before dying. Most of these wounds were fingernail imprints in the forearms, fingers, and thumbs. "Against an attack with hands one defends oneself with hands," the study explains. "The thumb grip is the strongest and most active part of the hand even in the act of strangulation and is therefore often subject to self-defense injuries."

The lack of injuries to both parties, then, probably meant that Bessie Goldberg had lost consciousness too quickly to put up much resistance—or to require much force to subdue. Whoever killed Bessie Goldberg must first have incapacitated her and then gone on to the uglier business of rape and strangulation. There is one very easy way to do that. It is called, among other things, the carotid takedown. When a person dies by strangulation—either by hanging, ligature, or manual compression of the neck—they usually do not die because the air supply to their lungs has been cut off; they die because blood supply to their brain has been cut off. This is merciful; at any given moment there are a couple of minutes' worth of air in the lungs, and death by asphyxiation is a slow and desperate process that can leave both victim and attacker covered in lacerations.

There is far less oxygen in the brain, however, and death by cerebral hypoxia—lack of oxygen to the brain—is correspondingly fast. Oxygen-bearing blood reaches the brain via the carotid arteries in the neck and leaves primarily through the jugular veins. Only eleven pounds of pressure to the carotid arteries are necessary to stop blood flow to the brain, and once the blood flow has stopped, the person loses consciousness in an average of ten seconds. A person who has lost consciousness because of constricted carotid arteries will regain consciousness in another ten seconds or so if the pressure is released. If pressure is not released, however, the unconscious person dies within minutes. As a result people have killed themselves by strangulation in the most benign-looking circumstances. They have hanged themselves from a bedpost while lying next to their sleeping spouse. (The weight of the head against the noose is enough to block the carotid artery.) They have hanged themselves while sitting on the floor. They have hanged themselves despite having a permanent tracheostomy—a breathing hole in their throat—that allowed a full supply of air to the lungs.

One can imagine that in order to tie a stocking around Bessie Goldberg's neck without sustaining wounds to his arms and face, the killer had to incapacitate her first, probably by cutting off blood flow in her carotid. He may have done this deliberately, or he may have done it unknowingly and been surprised by how quickly she lost consciousness. It takes considerable strength to crush someone's trachea, but it takes almost no effort to block their carotid arteries; the fact that Bessie Goldberg died with her glasses on suggests the latter. A small bone in her neck called the hyoid was also unbroken, which is extremely rare in elderly strangulation victims. In all likelihood, then, very little force was used to kill Bessie Goldberg. The killer almost certainly put her in a headlock from behind and squeezed her neck until she went limp.

The problem with the carotid takedown is that it works too well; numerous people have inadvertently been killed by police officers who were following proper procedure but didn't release their suspect in time. If Bessie Goldberg died in this way, it would have happened so quickly and silently that even someone in the next room might not have known. There is no history of sexual predation in Smith's past, and if he did indeed kill Bessie Goldberg, the experience may have been nearly as confusing to him as it was to her. Minutes earlier he was cleaning a white woman's house in suburban Belmont; now she was dead at his feet. His life as he knew it was over and another—undoubtedly worse—one was about to begin.

FIVE

THE FIRST ONE was found dead in her small Boston apartment on the evening of June 14, 1962. Her name was Anna Slesers, and she'd been clubbed on the back of the head and then strangled with the belt from her blue taffeta housecoat. No one knew that her murder would be the first of many, so her story merited only a few paragraphs in the *Boston Globe*. "An attractive divorcee was found strangled in her third-floor apartment at 77 Gainsboro Street [*sic*]," the article began. "Her son found Mrs. Anna Slesers, 55, on the kitchen floor when he came to take her to church. A cord was tightly knotted around her neck."

A dozen years earlier, Anna Slesers had fled with her two children to the United States from Latvia, where she had survived World War II in a camp for displaced people. She now lived on her own in a picturesque section of Boston known as Back Bay and worked as a factory seamstress for sixty dollars a week. She lived quietly and had virtually no social life; her primary interests were her children, her church, and classical music. On the evening of

June 14 her son, Juris, had planned to take her to the Latvian Lutheran Church in Roxbury, where services were held every year to mourn the day that the Soviet Army overran their country. Juris had showed up at seven o'clock, as they'd agreed, knocked on the apartment door, waited, pounded on it, waited some more, and then walked down to the street to check her mailbox. The mailbox was full, and he pulled the letters out of it and walked back upstairs. Forty-five minutes after he arrived, Juris put his thin shoulder to the door and broke it down with a couple of strong shoves.

He found his mother on the floor near the kitchen, grotesquely presented to whoever walked in next. A bathtub full of water was waiting for her, and an opera record, *Tristan und Isolde,* was turning silently on the phonograph. The first police officers to arrive thought that the death was a suicide, which prompted Juris to call his sister in Maryland with the bad news. For a divorced Latvian exile, the country's national day of mourning might be an appropriate day to decide you don't want to continue living. One of the officers who showed up later, however, immediately saw murder in the position of the body. Detective Jim Mellon of Boston Homicide guessed that Mrs. Slesers had been attacked in the bathroom and then dragged into the hallway on a small rug. There she had been strangled and probably raped. (The medical examiner later determined that in fact she'd been sexually assaulted with an object.)

Whoever had killed her had also taken great pains to pull open all the drawers in her bedroom dresser, as if looking for valuables, but had pointedly ignored her jewelry, her small gold watch, and the few dollars she had in her purse. Officer Mellon was annoyed by the fact that Juris had not covered up his mother's body before calling the police and decided that he was the one who had killed her. The theory did not advance very far. The police ultimately concluded that a burglar must have broken into the apartment, surprised Mrs. Slesers as she prepared to take a bath, and simply been overcome by "lust." He sexually assaulted her and then killed her to prevent being identified. There was roughly a murder a week in Boston, and the explanation for Mrs. Slesers's killing might have remained unquestioned if it hadn't happened again.

The next one came two weeks later: Nina Nichols, a sixty-eight-year-old widow who had just retired from a high-level hospital job, was found dead in her small Boston apartment on the evening of June 30. Her pink housecoat and slip had been yanked up to her waist, and she had been garroted with her own stockings, which the killer had then tied in a decorative bow. Like Anna Slesers, she had been sexually assaulted with an object, and the apartment had been thoroughly ransacked, though nothing—including a three-hundred-dollar camera—seemed to have been taken. There were also no signs of forced entry, and Nina Nichols's sister told the police that while they were speaking on the phone late that afternoon, her sister's doorbell had rung and Nichols had hung up in order to answer it. She never called back.

Nichols had been killed late in the day, and police detectives theorized that the murderer had rung doorbells randomly and decided to attack Mrs. Nichols because she was alone in the apartment. The *Boston Globe* noted that the killing was similar to that of Anna Slesers two weeks earlier, and quoted Lt. John Donovan, head of Boston Homicide, as saying that there was a "possibility" the same man had committed both murders. First thing Monday morning, Boston police commissioner Ed McNamara called a meeting of all department heads to discuss the murders.

By evening the people of Boston had little reason to doubt that it would be a long, murder-filled summer. Sixty-five-year-old Helen

Blake was found strangled by her own stockings in the working-class town of Lynn, and the manner of her death was by now sickeningly familiar. ANOTHER SILK STOCKING MURDER, the *Boston Globe* headlines shrieked on Tuesday morning. "A Lynn nurse was found strangled in her apartment under circumstances almost identical with the slaying of a Brighton woman 48 hours earlier." Helen Blake was a stout, modest woman who until recently had worked as a nurse at a local hospital. She was found facedown in her bed with two stockings and a bra wrapped tightly around her neck. The bra had been arranged in the cheerful bow that by now the police recognized as a signature of the killer. According to the autopsy, she was killed on the morning of June 30, the same day as Nina Nichols. Blake appeared to have been strangled in the kitchen and then carried to her bed and sexually assaulted with an object. She weighed 165 pounds, and police investigators concluded that only a powerful man could have picked her up and put her on the bed. The killer had also lugged a strongbox from under the bed to an armchair and tried pick the lock with a knife, but the tip of the blade had broken off in the keyhole.

The front door had a chain, a bolt, and a Yale lock, none of which had been tampered with, so Blake must have opened the door to her killer. Two bottles of fresh milk were found on top of her refrigerator, already gone sour in the summer heat. They had been delivered to her doorstep the morning of the murder, but if Blake had brought them in, she would have put them straight into the refrigerator. Could the killer have knocked on the door, presented her with the milk bottles, and then talked his way into the apartment? Would he have put them on top of the refrigerator before attacking her? Would he have then gone on to kill Nina Nichols in Boston later in the day, or was there another killer who had decided to imitate what he'd read in the papers about Anna Slesers?

"Since robbery is not the motive, we are dealing with a demented man," Dr. Richard Ford, head of the Department of Legal Medicine at Harvard University declared to the press. Ford was also the Suffolk County medical examiner, and he had called various law enforcement agencies together to try to solve what was quickly becoming a law enforcement crisis in Boston. "There is nothing to tie these crimes together, no single proof," he added. "The more such things happen, the more they are likely to happen because— and you can quote me—because the world is full of screwballs."

After Helen Blake there was a pause in the killings, and then in late August, an elderly Boston woman named Ida Irga was found in her apartment by the thirteen-year-old son of the building superintendent. The boy had gone in to check on her and had opened the door to find Mrs. Irga obscenely propped open on the living room floor. The date was Sunday, August 19, which meant that three out of four women had been killed on weekends. Did that mean that the killer had a weekday job? Ida Irga had a pillowcase knotted tightly around her throat and a foot wedged between the rungs of two separate chairs. It was, as one journalist explained it, a "grotesque parody" of a gynecological exam.

The similarities between the murdered women were startling. They were all elderly and lived alone on modest incomes. Most were affiliated with local hospitals in some way and listened to classical music. Without exception they were described by friends as well-groomed and punctual and led quiet, unexciting lives that were beyond moral reproach. They were all killed in a similar way and seemed to have let their murderer into their apartments voluntarily. Whoever the killer was, police thought that he had to be relatively benign looking and a very smooth talker. STRANGLER OF TWO A MOTHER-HATER? the *Boston Globe* headlines asked readers after the

Nichols murder. "A paranoid killer, obsessed with a mother-hate complex, was sought last night for the sex-crime strangulations of two women," the article explained. "All division commanders were ordered to compile a list of men . . . released from mental hospitals in the past year."

In the face of a horror that the police seemed unable to stop, a neat psychological explanation for why someone would want to rape and strangle old women must have reassured the public briefly. What many people did not realize, however, was that a diagnosis of the man's problems wouldn't be of much help if the suspect hadn't already gone through the system, and it wouldn't help at all if there were multiple killers whose violent impulses had finally been triggered by the Slesers murder. Then, just before the start of the Labor Day weekend, sixty-seven-year-old Jane Sullivan was found on her knees in a half-full bathtub, strangled with her own stockings.

The autopsy determined that Sullivan had been killed within twenty-four hours of Ida Irga, which meant that out of a total of five stranglings that summer, four had been committed within a day of one another. They came in pairs, in other words. Would several madmen, acting independently of one another, show any pattern to their killings? Probably not, unless they were reading about one another's crimes in the paper and then going out to copy them. In that case, however, the murders would be grouped within days of one another, not hours. The police were reluctant to acknowledge it, but the killings had started to look like the work of a lone madman who could not be stopped.

BOSTON PASSED THE fall of 1962 with plenty of murders but no more stranglings, and the police started to wonder whether the killer had been arrested for something else or had left the area or had simply stopped. The mechanism that starts people killing is a mysterious one that even the killers themselves don't fully understand, and it is capable of switching off as suddenly as it switches on. Maybe this particular person had killed enough women to satisfy whatever domination fantasy he'd been acting out. Maybe he'd hanged himself in his basement. Maybe he'd taken a break from his crimes in order to think up new, worse ones. There was no way to know.

Meanwhile the police were working furiously to follow up even the most outlandish leads. A special phone number was set up, DE 8-1212, to receive tips from the public. The unrelated strangling of a sixty-year-old white woman, found in a South Boston hotel room, further confused and terrified the public. (A man who had checked in to the room with her the night before was later convicted of the murder.) Within days of the murder of Helen Blake, every detective in Boston was ordered to work directly under the homicide bureau, and every robbery, vice, and narcotics inspector in the city was ordered to report to Lt. John Donovan. Known sex offenders were dragged into their local police station to be interrogated by three-man teams of detectives. Anyone discharged from a mental hospital in the past two years was similarly scrutinized. Police Commissioner Ed McNamara—brought in to straighten out a police department that had been thoroughly embarrassed by a CBS documentary called "Biography of a Bookie Joint"—issued advice to women who lived alone. He recommended that they double-lock their doors, lock their windows, and refuse entrance to anyone who did not identify himself on their doorstep. (The flaw in that advice, he soon realized, was that women would immediately open the door to anyone who identified himself as a police officer.) He also encouraged people in Boston to report any suspicious behavior to the Strangler hotline.

Police departments in Boston and outlying towns were predictably deluged with calls. A young woman reported that her boyfriend had tried to strangle her during a dispute, but a quick police investigation determined that the man couldn't have committed any of the murders. An older woman called a suburban police department to say that she was frightened and wanted a police officer sent over to keep her company; the police declined. One woman reported that her phone rang, and when she picked it up, a voice said, "This is the Strangler, you're next." A neighbor of Nina Nichols, who was killed in late June, reported having seen a white man sitting in a car and looking up at Nichols's apartment for three Saturdays in a row before the murder. Nothing came of it. A woman was raped by an ex-marine she met in a bar who told her, while raping her, that he liked to choke older women. A Brockton housewife opened her front door, expecting a friend, and was greeted by an unknown man. She fell dead of fright before he could explain that he was an encyclopedia salesman.

Police investigators went through every diary, notebook, and scrap of paper in the apartments of the dead women for names and phone numbers. Each one then had to be tracked down and investigated. Detectives took latent fingerprints from the crime scenes and then compared them to other crime scenes to see if anyone came up twice. They worked their way through routine checks of some six thousand people who knew the deceased or lived near the deceased or had simply attracted someone's attention near one of the crime scenes. Much was made of the fact that all the women were in some way associated with hospitals, until it was pointed out that health care and nursing were among the few professions easily accessible to women, and moreover, that elderly people of both sexes would be likely to have links to hospitals.

The FBI was brought in to give a seminar on sexual perversion, and investigators gradually put together a psychological profile of the kind of person who might be driven to kill and sodomize elderly women. Since most of the murders happened around dusk or on weekends, it was thought that the killer might have a nine-to-five job in the Boston area, and that he killed when he wasn't working, or on his way home at the end of the day. His job, one psychiatrist hypothesized, was a menial one, possibly at a hospital. Since several of the murders took place in or near the Back Bay—known for its concentration of artists and bohemians—some suggested that the killer might be homosexual. Or he might be a man dressed as a woman—which would explain his ability to get women to open their doors to him. Or maybe he was just a woman, period. A local psychiatrist consulted by the police decided that the murders "were palpably the work of a homosexual. They could have been done by a woman homosexual—one who through frustration or emotional upheaval develops a hatred of her sex. If a male homosexual was the killer, he probably had a hatred of his mother or some other older woman who dominated his childhood, and he now gets his satisfaction from the defiling of older women's bodies."

It didn't require a degree in psychology to theorize that a man who molested and killed older women might harbor a grudge against his mother. Such was the level of terror in Boston, however, that even an insight as vague and obvious as that one could still make it to the front page of the papers. It was right around that time—the fall of 1962—that my mother had her first experience with the workman named Al.

SIX

ELLEN JUNGER, Belmont, Massachusetts:
"It was quite early. I heard the bulkhead door slam, and I heard him go downstairs, I was still in my nightgown and bathrobe, and I hadn't gotten dressed yet. I heard him come in, and two or three minutes later I heard him call me. So I opened the door to the cellar, and I saw him down there at the foot of the stairs and he was looking at me. And he was looking in a way that is almost indescribable. He had this intense look in his eyes, a strange kind of burning in his eyes, as if he was almost trying to hypnotize me. As if by sheer force of will he could draw me down into that basement."

My mother knew almost nothing about Al at this point; it was only two or three days into the job, and they had never even been alone together. She stood at the top of the stairs looking into Al's eyes and wondering what to do. What is it, Al? she finally said.

There's something the matter with your washing machine, he told her.

My mother thought about that. Al had been in the house only a

43

couple of minutes and the washing machine wasn't even on. Why was he worrying about it? He was supposed to be outside building a studio, not in our basement worrying about the appliances. It didn't make sense. Clearly he wanted to get her down into the basement, and clearly if she did that things could go very wrong. My mother told him that she was busy, and then she closed the basement door and shot the bolt.

A few moments later she heard the bulkhead door bang shut and the sound of Al's car starting up. He drove off and did not come back for the rest of the day. My mother didn't tell my father about the incident because she was afraid he would overreact and cause a scene, but she decided that when she saw Russ Blomerth the next morning, she would tell him she didn't want Al working on the property anymore. The next morning my father left for work and this time the whole crew showed up for work—Mr. Wiggins, Russ Blomerth, and Al. My mother got ready to confront Blomerth, but when she saw Al, he was so friendly and cheerful— "Hi, Mrs. Junger, good morning, how are you?"—that she hesitated. Was she overreacting? Did she really want to get a man fired for the look in his eyes?

Al had a wife and two children to support, and in the end my mother didn't say anything. She decided to wait a few days and see how things went. The weather was already cold when the crew poured the foundation, and the first thing Blomerth did was erect a wood frame over the work site and cover it with heavy plastic tarpaulins. That way they could keep the cement warm with diesel heaters so that it would cure properly. Al dropped by every day to fill the heaters with diesel, and once the foundation was finished, all three men showed up to start framing out the walls and roof. Blomerth and Wiggins were the expert builders, and Al was the laborer of the crew, the heavy lifter. "He wasn't much taller than I am, but he was absolutely the strongest man I ever saw," my mother remembers. "I mean, he wasn't muscle bound, he was just strong. I don't think he was wildly intelligent but he was clever. No, 'clever' isn't the right word. He knew his way around."

The work on the studio stopped over the holidays, though Al came out every day to fuel the heaters. One bitter night he stopped by as usual, but this time he brought his four-year-old son, Michael, and his eight-year-old daughter, Judy. Al finished with the heaters and then came in to introduce his children to my father, who was sick in bed with the flu. My father was born in Germany and had an accent, and Al said that if he spoke to Judy in German, she would understand because her mother was German as well. My father said a few words to her, and then Al wished him well and took his children back out of the house and drove away. My father still didn't know about the incident in the cellar, and it occurred to him that Al's last name, which was DeSalvo, meant "safe" in Italian, and that it was a fitting last name for someone who seemed so solid and dependable.

That was the only time that Al was ever in the house, although occasionally my mother would go out to the studio and have lunch with him when he was there on his own. Al never gave her the sort of look he had in the cellar that day—a "bold male look," as my mother described it to my father years later—but there was still something about him that made my mother uneasy. She gave private art lessons at home, and every week a teenager named Marie came by in the afternoon to learn to draw. One afternoon Marie arrived before my mother, and she let herself in to the newly finished studio to wait. It was a warm day, and she was dressed in a madras shift, and Al must have noticed her through the plate-glass windows because the next thing she knew, he was standing next to her. You must be the model, he said.

Marie was sixteen years old and easily embarrassed. Oh no, I'm just the student, she said. Al put his arm around her waist and pulled her close. But your waist is so small, you've *got* to be the model, he insisted. Marie struggled between feeling flattered that an older man was paying attention to her and terrified that it was a form of attention she couldn't stop. Right at the point when she began worrying what was going to happen next, my mother walked in. There's Ellen! she said and broke from Al's weird hug. She ran over to my mother and told her what had happened, and my mother got her settled at her easel and then went outside and told Al that she didn't like what she had heard.

Aw, she's just a kid, she's so cute, Al said. I just wanted to hug her.

My mother told him that she didn't want anything like that to ever happen again. It was the last time she left Marie alone in the house with Al.

The studio was finished in mid-March, the day after Bessie Goldberg was murdered. There are photographs, however, of the studio with an open metal toolbox on the roof and an oak tree fully leafed out in the background. That means that some sort of work went on into May, though my mother's memory is that Al was not involved. My mother's memory is that the day after Bessie Goldberg was killed, Russ Blomerth took the photograph of his crew and my mother and me in the finished studio, and then Al left the job for good. The studio had a flagstone entry and a lovely winter garden that took in sunlight from the southwest through floor-to-ceiling French doors. It had a tile floor and big triangular windows in the eaves and a domed Plexiglas skylight that brightened the room even in midwinter. Along the south wall my mother set up her big wooden easel, and along the east wall she had a worktable with a glass top on which she could mix her colors. Marie continued to come in the afternoons for lessons, and I have dim memories of her struggling with charcoal and paper while my mother simultaneously kept an eye on me and on her and got dinner going in the kitchen.

SEVEN

BELMONT WAS CARVED in 1859 from lands formerly belonging to neighboring towns in an area of upland meadow and forest that once belonged to the Pequuset Indians. Early Belmont was a rugged little outpost laced with old Indian footpaths that connected the fields and boggy meadows where colonists grazed their cattle. Fish weirs were built on the Charles River, gravel operations were started in the numerous deposits of glacial till, and, in winter, ice was cut from the kettle ponds that had been left behind when the glaciers retreated from Massachusetts Bay thirteen thousand years ago. Belmont owed its existence as a modern town to a railroad that was built westward from Cambridge in the 1840s. Decades earlier a young Boston merchant named Frederick Tudor had started cutting ice out of a large glacier-formed pond called Fresh Pond and selling it to Bostonians. In order to sell ice all year round, Tudor started packing his ice in sawdust, and that worked so well that he was soon shipping Fresh Pond ice to the West Indies. The costs of moving so much ice by horse and cart to the Boston waterfront were prohibitive, so Tudor built a railroad that was eventually extended to what was then known as Wellington Hill Station.

A village formed around the railway station, roads were built to the village, and newcomers built homes along the roads. Within a decade the community that had formed around Wellington Hill started clamoring for recognition. It was finally incorporated in 1859 and named after Bellmont, an English-style estate built by the town's top taxpayer, John Cushing. With cool summer breezes on the hill, light industry on the flats, and a railroad line running straight into Boston, it became one of the first bedroom communities in the country. Wellington Hill was renamed Belmont Hill, and its rocky sheep pastures became some of the most sought-after real estate in the Boston area. It was on the outermost flanks of Belmont Hill, within earshot of Route 2, that Israel Goldberg bought a modest colonial-style house in 1951.

Belmont has always been known for its careful conservatism, and the early town planners reinforced that idea as strongly as possible with the civic buildings that grew up around what was now called Belmont Center. The town hall is a massive 1880s brick-and-slate-roof structure with numerous towers, chimneys, and cupolas. The railroad station behind it was built with fieldstone walls thick enough to take cannonballs. The police station, built in the 1930s, is a no-nonsense Georgian revival–style with end chimneys, granite trim, and a pedimented entry that created—in the words of one town publication—a "dignified building as the center of law enforcement in Belmont."

It was into that dignified building that Roy Smith was led in handcuffs on the afternoon of March 12, 1963.

———

"WHAT IS YOUR name?"

"Roy Smith."

"Where do you live, Roy?"

"One seventy-five Northampton Street, Boston."

"Did you come out to Belmont yesterday?"

"I did."

"Did you go to the Massachusetts Unemployment Service yesterday looking for work?"

"Yes, before I came out here."

"Before you came out here?"

"Yes. That's where I got work."

"And where did they send you?"

"Fourteen Scott Street. I think it's Scott. Yes, 14 Scott Street, I believe."

"Whom did you talk with at the bureau who gave you this job to come out here?"

"Mrs. Martin."

"And she sent you out here to this address?"

"Yes, she sent me out here. I don't know whether it's out 'here.' I don't know where I'm at now."

Roy Smith was in a chair in a back room of the Belmont police station. A stenographer named Berta Shear was recording every word that was said. Gathered around Smith were Chief Paul Robinson, two additional Belmont police officers, a detective from the state police barracks, and a lieutenant detective from the police barracks named John Cahalane. Cahalane was the highest-ranking officer in the room and was sent by the Middlesex County District Attorney's Office because of the grave implications of the case. Eventually the DA himself, John Droney, showed up. Bessie Goldberg's murder was not just another killing; it was the ninth in a series of brutal sex slayings, and the authorities were still not sure that Bessie Goldberg was the only woman Smith had killed.

The interrogation started off with Chief Robinson and Lieutenant Maguire of the Belmont police asking Smith to tell them, step by step, what he had done the morning before. Smith said he took the bus to Belmont, asked directions at a local gas station and arrived at the Goldberg house just before noon. He said that Bessie Goldberg made him a bologna sandwich for lunch and then showed him what to clean after he'd finished eating. He said he cleaned the couch and the floors and the windows. He said he cleaned what he thought was the library—"it had a lot of books in it"—and the living room and the dining room. He said that he was paid six dollars and thirty cents—a dollar fifty an hour for four hours, plus thirty cents' bus fare—and that he left around a quarter to four. He said he knew the time because he happened to see a wall clock when he went into the pharmacy to buy his cigarettes.

This must have struck the investigators as odd. Not only did Smith have the time wrong by almost an hour—the pharmacy clerk, among other people, placed the time at just after three—but if he was bending the truth in order to cover his guilt, he was bending it in the wrong direction; Smith was placing himself at the murder scene for the maximum amount of time possible. Israel Goldberg had said that he called his wife around two-thirty and then arrived home just before four. If you were Roy Smith and you were guilty, you would say that you left just after the phone call and that in the intervening hour and twenty minutes, someone else must have sneaked into the house and killed Bessie Goldberg. But in Smith's version there was only a ten-minute window for someone else to have committed the crime.

If the police were puzzled by this tactic—or lack thereof—they didn't show it, they just continued prodding him. Smith said that after buying cigarettes at the pharmacy, he got on what he thought was the bus back to Cambridge, but it was going in the wrong direction. Instead of getting off he rode to the end of the line, smoked a cigarette with the driver during the five-minute layover, and then rode back to Harvard Square. He said that he left a card with his landlady's phone number on Bessie Goldberg's kitchen counter in case she wanted more work, and that he worked for a lot of different people and that they were all pleased with his work and wanted him to come back to clean for them, and that he had a wallet full of phone numbers to prove it.

"I ain't hurt nobody, nothing like that," he added.

"You what?" Chief Robinson said.

"I haven't hurt nobody, I'm not like that, I take nothing from nobody."

"Why do you say you've never hurt anybody?"

"I haven't, I haven't. I mean this guy here—"

"Will you repeat that, Roy?"

Before Smith could answer, Lieutenant Cahalane of the state police stepped in. "Do you want a drink of water, Roy?"

"Yes, please," Roy answered. "When this guy come down here at this girl's house he had a pistol all in my face, you know what I mean."

"Why didn't you go back to your house in Boston?"

"Why didn't I go?"

"Yes."

"Because I was drunk and I was still drinking and I was drinking when the police come by there, I sure was. And besides, I mean, I stay by myself anyway. . . . I got my own place, four rooms, you know, I go there when I get ready."

"Roy, what happened there?" Cahalane finally asked. "Now give us the whole story."

"Beg pardon?"

"Give us the whole story of what happened in that living room."

"I told you, I told you."

"You're holding something back."

"Mister, I've been working my whole life, you understand. I never put my hand on nobody. . . . I ain't did nothing but drinking, so—"

"You weren't drunk when you landed in Belmont yesterday morning, were you, at twelve o'clock noon?"

"Of course not, I got drinking last night."

"You know what you did out on Scott Road yesterday?"

"You all got the wrong man."

"Why did you do it?"

"You got the wrong man, you can't pin all that stuff on me, I ain't did nothing. I ain't did nothing to that woman yesterday in Belmont and no other Belmont and no other place. Look, I love myself, do you understand? I love myself. I ain't going to stick my neck out—you kidding?"

Smith's only demonstrable departure from the complete truth came soon afterward, when he was asked about the name "Bell" on his mailbox. Smith claimed that it was the previous tenant, who was still getting his mail there; in fact it referred to Carol Bell, who had been his girlfriend and was the mother of his son, whom he called "Scooter." Carol Bell had left him five days earlier without any forwarding address. Carol Bell had sent Smith to prison for six months for nonpayment of child support. Carol Bell, in other words, was not a chapter of Smith's life that he would want the police to know about. Smith did, however, mention that there was another tenant in the building, a woman named Blackstone.

"You are a male, aren't you, Roy?" Cahalane asked.

"What?"

"Are you a male—sex?"

"I'm a male."

"You don't use sanitary napkins, do you?"

Smith addressed the other officers: "I don't know what he's talking about now."

"Do you wear women's clothes?"

"No."

"Who do the women's clothes belong to?"

"Blackstone. What about her clothes?"

Smith was refusing to admit to the murder, but neither could the police catch him in a significant lie. Much of a police interrogation consists of asking otherwise meaningless details about a suspect's day that he can't possibly keep track of. Once the police have opened up even a small contradiction in the testimony, they have a way into the web of lies that inevitably surrounds any denial of guilt. In the eyes of the police Smith was so obviously guilty that his refusal to make everyone's life easier by confessing seemed to exasperate them. They were playing their parts, in a sense, but Smith was not playing his. Again it was Lieutenant Cahalane who attempted to break through the denials.

"Straighten me out, will you? I'm all mixed up."

"Go ahead," said Smith. Cahalane proceeded to introduce himself and everyone else in the room, including the stenographer. He then led Smith once again through every detail of his morning. He asked what time Smith woke up, what he ate for breakfast, where he got off the bus. With slow, grinding thoroughness he asked exactly what work Smith performed in the Goldberg house, which rooms he worked in, and how long everything took. He asked what door he entered through, what door he left through, and whom he saw on the short walk to the bus station. At one point Cahalane asked if he saw three children walking along the sidewalk on Pleasant Street—Dougie Dreyer and his friends coming home from school—and Smith said that he did. The children all placed Smith leaving the crime scene, and Smith would have known that, but he still declined to fall into the trap of lying. Cahalane was getting nowhere.

"Do you ever black out?" Cahalane finally asked.

"I never blacked out in my life."

"Do you ever find yourself getting into some sort of predicament that you don't remember getting into?"

"No."

"You know at all times everything you're doing?"

"Sure, yes—I mean I'm normal, if that's what you mean."

"You have never been in any mental hospital?"

"No."

"Have you ever fainted in the street?"

"Never."

Cahalane was trying to lure Smith into a legal trap. If he killed Bessie Goldberg but didn't remember doing it, then it could not possibly be premeditated. The definition of first-degree murder is the killing of another human being "with malice aforethought," and a blackout would effectively remove intentionality from the crime, reducing the charge to manslaughter. Had Smith taken the bait and acknowledged that perhaps he *had* killed her without realizing it, he almost certainly would have been destroyed at trial, but that was not Cahalane's problem.

"This was a pretty nice lady?"

"She was nice."

"She treated you nice?"

"Real nice."

"Did you proposition her?"

"No, sir."

"Did you ask her to be over-friendly?"

"Never."

"Listen, Roy, no one is trying to put you in the middle, we're just trying to find out what happened."

"Look, this is serious; I'm giving it to you straight," said Smith. "If you'll excuse me for saying this here, there's too many women out there for me to be making a proposition for somebody. Do you think I want my neck broken?"

"You didn't ask her to be extra friendly?"

"No, I'd swear on a stack of Bibles as high as a building, I swear."

"Did you make a grab at her when she refused you?"

"I never made no passes at her."

"Roy, that's not very reasonable, I'm telling you."

"I didn't make no passes. That lady never made no passes at me. She was nice. She fixed me dinner [lunch] and got me a cup of tea. I sat down and ate that and got right back up like I do in everyone's house. I got right back up and started working."

"Roy, something happened in that house, and it is quite natural that we should feel you are responsible."

"Why me?"

"Because you were the only one who was there. Don't you understand? If there is nobody else there but you and the woman and something happens to the woman, naturally we got to think you did it. Now listen, Roy, nobody is trying to put you in the middle. If there is something bothering you and you made a grab for her, all you have to do is say so."

"I didn't."

"It's no big mystery, it happens every day."

"I'm telling you, you can take a knife and take my insides out—you can take me to a hospital and let them do anything to me."

"I'm not going to do anything—all I want to know is what happened."

"How do I know? I went there, and I worked for that woman. She's not the only woman I worked for."

"I believe—they tell me—you're a good worker."

"Jesus Christ, take me to a hospital, let them do anything to me."

"Listen Roy—at the time this happened to the woman—"

"Yes?"

"—that somebody knocked her flat—"

"I haven't knocked nobody flat."

"I'm telling you; you listen."

"Okay."

"At the time somebody attacked this woman you were the only one in the house, so naturally we have to figure that you were the one who attacked her. Now, are you the one who attacked her or not?"

"Yes, someone's got to get blamed for it."

"No, I didn't figure that. That is why we're talking to you. We don't want to put anything on you—all I want is the truth."

"There's got to be some kind of way you all could see whether I'm lying or not."

"That's what we're trying to figure out," said Cahalane. "If something happened accidentally, all you have got to do is say so. If she were standing on a table or chair and fell off and you grabbed her all you got to do—"

"Do you mind if I say something?"

"I don't mind."

One can imagine Smith drawing himself up for this. The police have asked Smith to step into their shoes for a moment; now Smith was doing the same. "My home is in Mississippi," Smith said. "There's no way I'd take no white woman because I love my neck, you understand?"

"But this is the North, not the South," Cahalane answered.

"I know that too."

"You have a lot more freedom up here."

"I'm telling you one thing: I ain't going to take no one's woman, Jesus Christ, especially a white woman, you kidding? I've got more sense than that, Jesus Christ."

"But still, the woman was lying on the floor, wasn't she?"

"No sir—"

"What?"

"That woman wasn't touched when I left there, no sirree. If I touched that woman do you think I'd be still messing around here? Are you kidding? I ain't touched no woman. Maybe somebody come by after I left."

"You have something more to tell us, you're holding something back."

"All right, then, you say I got something to tell you. Then all right. I ain't got nothing."

"Roy, let's have it."

"All right," Smith says. "Go ahead, have it."

For a black man in a police station in 1963 to speak sarcastically to his interrogators regarding the rape and murder of a white woman must have been rare indeed, even in Massachusetts. Back home in Mississippi it could have gotten him killed. "You've been lying all afternoon here, for the last half hour," said Maguire. "Now you're smart enough to know that science is going to trip you up."

"Not going to trip me up."

"So why don't you start now and give us the right story and get it off your mind? It's bothering you."

"Nothing bothering me myself because—I ain't did nothing and I'm not afraid of nothing myself. Y'all do just whatever you want but I'm telling you I ain't did nothing."

At this point Smith asked Chief Robinson for a cigarette, who gave him one. Maguire took the opportunity to interject, "Get it off your chest, Roy, let's have it."

"I'm not no Strangler here, are you kidding?" Smith said. "Shit."

There must have been silence in the room. There must have been glances between the police officers. "Who said anything about being the Strangler?" Maguire finally said.

"That's what ya'll are trying to put on me. I seen that guy from the paper up there, people taking all the pictures and stuff out there, putting me on TV—you go ahead on and try to prove that stuff, go ahead on—"

"We will prove it."

"Go ahead, do anything you want," Smith said. "You know better than that. Me, I don't go around and kill somebody."

The interrogation of Roy Smith went on into the early hours of March 13. After twelve hours of questioning, Smith still refused to admit his guilt, and the police had no choice but to let the district attorney take over. In the meantime, an ambitious young Boston lawyer named Beryl Cohen agreed to take Smith's case pro bono. Cohen had been alerted to Smith's plight by a reporter friend of his named Gene Pell, who had staked out the Belmont police station for what was supposed to be a Boston Strangler story. As the hours dragged by, though, Pell had started to worry that Smith's legal rights were not being protected, and so he called Cohen, who in turn tracked down Dorothy Hunt. It was Hunt who gave Cohen the go-ahead to represent Smith.

On March 21 a Middlesex County grand jury found that Roy Smith "did assault and beat Bessie Goldberg with intent to kill and murder her, and by such assault and beating did kill and murder said Bessie Goldberg." He was not charged with any of the other Boston stranglings because he had been in prison for most of the previous year and could not have committed them. When asked by the judge how he pleaded, Smith answered in a strong, clear voice, "I plead mute." (Pleading mute was a way for Smith to avoid admitting guilt while still keeping his options open.) Smith was remanded to Bridgewater State Prison for psychiatric observation, and a trial date was set for the following November.

EIGHT

L.C. MANNING SITS in a trash-filled pickup truck in his driveway in Oxford, Mississippi, sweating in the heavy April heat. In the late fifties he was arrested by Sheriff Boyce Bratton for public drinking and wound up in the Oxford City jail, where he got into a fight with another inmate. Not only did the other inmate lose the fight, but he was also white, for which Manning spent a year's forced labor at Parchman Farm. He was there about a decade after Roy, though things hadn't changed much. Manning has big wide hands that sit obediently on his lap when he talks, and powerful shoulders that must have served him well when he was young. They must have served him well in prison. Manning is old enough to remember when Roy got arrested for stealing cotton. Manning is old enough to remember Oxford's last lynching. Manning is old enough to remember getting flogged by a white man. Parchman was bad, he says but so was everything else. It didn't begin and end at the prison gate.

"Oh, man, you don't know shit," he says, shaking his head.

Manning lives in a patched-together house on the outskirts of Oxford. There is a toolshed in Manning's backyard made entirely of discarded wooden doors. "It were hell down there, that's why I don't take no shit now. If I go again I want to go for something I actually *did*. But with the help of Jesus and God I seen 'em *all* go down below. I ain't jokin'—Bratton, Old Judge McElroy, all of 'em, and thank Jesus I still here. Three people you put your trust in: Jesus, the Lord, and yourself. Trust no man."

Parchman occupies forty-six square miles of snake-infested bayous and flatlands in the Yazoo Delta, which stretches along the Mississippi River from Vicksburg to Memphis and east to the Chickasaw Ridge. Parts of the farm were blessed with rich alluvial soil known as "buckshot" that ran up to fifty feet deep, and other parts were so swampy and tangled that they had turned back Union troops toward the end of the Civil War. The prison had no fence around it because it was too big and no central cell blocks because the inmates were distributed around the plantation in work camps. Every morning at four thirty, the inmates were woken up by a bell and marched out to the fields, where they worked from sunup until sundown. The plowing was done by mule, and the picking was done by hand. At dark the men marched back to the work camp and ate a dinner prepared by other inmates. Every work camp had a vegetable garden and livestock pen, and the inmates subsisted almost entirely off what they could grow and raise. After dinner the lights were turned out and the men went to sleep, and at four thirty the next morning it started all over again. There were men who passed their entire lives that way.

Flogging was the primary method of enforcing discipline at Parchman and was not officially banned until 1971. A leather strap known as Black Annie was used liberally on anyone who would not work, anyone who disobeyed a direct order, anyone who displayed anything approaching impudence. An escape attempt merited something called a "whipping without limits," which—since there was virtually no medical care at Parchman in the early days—was effectively a death sentence. Inmates also died in knife fights, died in their bunk beds of malaria and pneumonia and tuberculosis, and sometimes just dropped dead of heatstroke in the fields. It was the closest thing to slavery that the South had seen since the Civil War.

The result of this relentless brutality was that Parchman was almost completely self-sufficient—and extremely profitable. In addition to growing food to eat and cotton to sell, the inmates also maintained a brickworks, a sawmill, a cotton gin, a sewing shop, a slaughterhouse, a shoe shop, a machine shop, and a thirty-man carpentry crew on the farm. During Roy's time Parchman was turning a profit of around a million dollars a year, mostly from cotton sales. In the interest of high production, conjugal visits were allowed for the black inmates, and every Sunday wives and prostitutes were brought out to the work camps. As one camp sergeant explained to an investigator in 1963, "If you let a nigger have some on Sunday, he will really go out and do some work for you on Monday." The wives arrived by train on weekends, and the prostitutes lived in one of the administrative buildings. The inmates met their women in a rough shack they called the "Red House" or the "Tonk," and were limited to forty-five minutes at a time. If they went over forty-five minutes they lost their conjugal privileges for two weeks.

Regular inmates like Roy were called "gunmen" because they worked under the eye of mounted guards who carried .30-30 Winchester rifles across their knees. The guards were called "trusty-shooters" and were chosen from the prison population; they were usually the most violent inmates who had life sentences and nothing to lose. They wore wide-striped uniforms with the stripes running vertically, and the rest of the inmates wore uniforms with the stripes running horizontally. They were called "up-and-downs" and "ring-rounds," respectively. In the odd logic of the prison world, the same act that put a shooter in prison in the first place—murder—could also win his release. When the gunmen walked out into the fields to begin work, the shooters drew a "gun line" in the dirt and sat up on their horses and waited. If a man set foot over the gun line, the shooter shouted a warning and then shot to kill. The same was true if the convict got closer than twenty feet to a shooter or failed to wait for permission to cross the gun line in order to relieve himself. A shooter who killed an escaping convict was often rewarded with a pardon from the governor and released from prison. In a state that had no parole laws until 1944, it wasn't a bad deal.

The violence in Parchman was so extreme—and the inmate population so disproportionately black—that it is hard not to see the entire Mississippi penal system simply as revenge against blacks for the South's defeat in the Civil War. Three years before Roy was locked up, two fourteen-year-old black boys were executed by the state of Mississippi for murdering a white man; the boys had been indicted, tried, and convicted all in less than twenty-four hours. And as Roy was chopping cotton in Parchman's dusty fields, another terrible scandal was unfolding. In 1945 a black man named Willie McGee had been arrested for raping a white woman named Willametta Hawkins in the small town of Laurel. McGee, an extremely handsome man who had a wife and four young children, was arrested for the crime and held incommunicado for a month before being tried and sentenced to death. The jury had deliberated two and a half minutes to decide his fate.

In the end McGee would almost have been better off if he actually *had* raped Willametta Hawkins. For the tormented white psyche of that era, the only thing worse than a black man forcing himself on a white woman was a black man *not* forcing himself on a white woman, and that was apparently what had happened. McGee's good looks had caught the attention of Willametta Hawkins several years earlier, despite the fact that she was married and had a newborn child. She offered him a job that he quickly accepted, and once he was working for her, Willametta maneuvered him into having an affair by threatening to claim rape if he ever turned her down. After three years of furtive sex McGee finally managed to end the affair, and, true to her word, Willametta told her husband and then went to the police. It didn't take them long to track down Willie McGee.

Roy was out of prison eight months when the state of Mississippi executed McGee. The U.S. Supreme Court had stayed McGee's execution three times to no avail. After the streetlights dimmed in Laurel, Mississippi, every black man in the state must have seen every white woman he knew as a potential threat to his freedom, if not his life, and decided that the safest strategy was to avoid them at all costs. When Roy Smith said to Lieutenant Cahalane in the basement of the Belmont police station, "My home is in Mississippi—there's no way I'd take no white woman," he was very possibly thinking of Willie McGee. That same year a black sharecropper in North Carolina was charged with attempted rape for merely *looking* at a white woman. He was acquitted by a hung jury, but the message to black men in America was clear: If you even *think* about it, you're dead.

Technically McGee's death was not a lynching, it was an execution. In the decades following the Civil War, more than four thousand black men were lynched in the former Confederate states, but by Roy Smith's time, public lynchings had mostly given way to quasi-legal death sentences. (One notable exception happened in Oxford in 1935, when a mob broke into the city jail and lynched a black man named Elwood Higginbotham. He was killed while a jury was still debating his case in the courthouse across the street.) Between 1930 and 1964, 455 men were executed for rape in the United States. Most of them were black, and most of them were accused of raping white women. A black man accused of rape was a stand-in for his entire race, and he was lynched—or executed by the state—because a gradual mingling of the races had started to occur that racist whites were powerless to stop. Ultimately the purpose of lynching was not to dispense justice but to control the black population. Since lynching was primarily an instrument of terror, it mattered little whether the accused were guilty or not—in some ways killing an innocent man made even more of an impression than killing a guilty one—and the more gruesome the killing, the more terror it spread. As white power in the South gradually waned after the Civil War, lynchings inevitably attained a savagery that may have shocked even some of the perpetrators.

In an 1899 case that became infamous throughout the South, a young black man named Sam Hose was burned alive in front of several thousand people, many of them Christians who had left their church services early to enjoy the spectacle. The ringleaders chained Hose to a tree, cut off his ears, poured kerosene on him, and then lit a match. When he finally stopped writhing, the crowd rushed forward and cut pieces from his smoldering body. When that was gone, they chopped up the tree he was chained to, and when that was gone, they attacked the chain itself. Later that day, spectators were spotted walking through town waving pieces of bone and charred flesh. Hose's knuckles turned up at a local grocery store.

Hose's murder and many others like it warped the minds of an entire generation of blacks. So many blacks fled the South because of the threat of mob justice that farm owners began to have trouble finding workers for their fields. The South's relationship with public torture culminated in 1937, when two black men were accused of murdering a white store owner in the town of Duck Hill, Mississippi. Duck Hill is about seventy-five miles from Oxford. The men were abducted by a mob on the courthouse steps and taken to some woods outside town where a crowd of several hundred men, women, and children had gathered. The accused would not confess to the crime—there was absolutely no evidence they'd had anything to do with it—so they were whipped with chains and then tortured with a blowtorch. Unable to withstand the pain, one of the men finally admitted to the killing and was quickly rewarded by being shot to death. His companion held out until his eyes were gouged out with a pickax and then he, too, confessed. He was finally doused with gasoline and burned alive.

Roy Smith was nine years old when Duck Hill happened. It was one of the last public lynchings in America, but it clearly demonstrated that the white race was still a kind of third rail, and that if you were black and happened to touch it when it was on, you were dead. The deadly voltage of race continued to kill—more covertly—throughout the thirties and forties, but things were slowly changing. In 1951 the Civil Rights Congress, headed by a black man named William Patterson, submitted to the United Nations a document titled *We Charge Genocide,* which described the treatment of blacks in America in terms drawn straight from the Nuremberg trials of World War II. The word "genocide" was newly minted then, and extremely potent. Patterson made an eloquent case that extrajudicial violence, police and prosecutorial misconduct, and economic injustice against blacks amounted to an attempt to "destroy, in whole or in part, a national, ethnical, racial or religious group." The group they referred to was the fifteen million Americans with African blood in their veins, and the attempt to destroy that group violated the same international laws, Patterson claimed, that had been used to prosecute Nazi war criminals several years earlier.

Patterson accused the United States of violating the 1948 Genocide Convention, the Universal Declaration of Human Rights, the United Nations Charter, and the Fourteenth and Fifteenth Amendments to the U.S. Constitution. He delivered his petition simultaneously to the Fifth Session of the UN General Assembly in Paris and to the office of the secretary general in New York. Any doubt of complicity by the federal government was erased in 1949, when Congress abandoned a bill that would have made lynching a federal crime. Heavily pressured by the United States, the UN never responded to Patterson's charges. Roy Smith undoubtedly did not know that such an eloquent document was arguing for his rights in far-off cities, but it probably wouldn't have mattered much to him anyway. Soon after getting out of Parchman, Roy Smith voted, as they say, with his feet. He joined the hundreds of thousands of young blacks who streamed out of the former Confederate states, heading north.

NINE

"ROY SMITH JUST liked to have fun, we was all young and naturally we drinked—quite a bit of drinkin', in fact. Mostly Seagram's, I believe, Seven Crown, beer, stuff like that. Roy would work but he wasn't no steady man, sort of go place to place, more or less work on cars and stuff. Wild, drinkin', that was what he liked to do, he liked to have fun. 'Course I was married a long time 'fore me and Roy got together. He liked women, he *loved* women, he never did get married that I know of, but he had lots of women, never did hang on, that's the way he was, never had no particular one."

James Jenkins is Roy's uncle on his mother's side. He is a small, dignified man who lives near the airport in South Memphis with his wife, Arizona. As a teenager Arizona fasted for three days and was visited by the Lord in her own living room and started testifying on the spot, and she has been testifying ever since. She and James have had had fourteen children, though one of their sons was killed by a drug dealer who broke into his apartment and shot him with a .357 Magnum. He was trying to kill someone else.

When Roy was young he spent some time with James in Memphis, and he immediately fell in love with Arizona's sister. The sister was nineteen years old and spent six months making promises to Roy while simultaneously trying to keep her husband from finding out. Her husband finally tracked Roy down and had a conversation with him that involved at least one knife, and after that the affair ended and Roy left Memphis for good. Working odd jobs, Roy followed his uncle to Wayne, Michigan, and then to Detroit and finally to Chicago. Uncle and nephew wound up on the West Side living together and working in restaurants together and drinking together and fighting together. According to James, they could get into a fight just walking down the street and looking at someone wrong.

"One time I got into a theater, and this white guy behind me put his feet up cross the seat back," James recalls of one particularly memorable evening out with Roy. "I turned and I said, 'I don't think it right you putting your feet up in my face,' and so he said, 'I'll tell you what—when you move 'em them I'll let 'em be moved,' so I looked around to see where he was at and when he wasn't payin' no 'tention I was on him. I jump over the seat and tried to knock his face off, but I didn't know what I'd grabbed; he just stood up and I'd grabbed a paratrooper. Man, he was so much bigger 'n me, I could feel all that weight, and I can't turn him loose now, and then his friends all get into it, and they turned the lights on and everything, they pulled me offa him and kicked me out. Roy said, 'Let's go back in there,' and I said, 'Are you crazy?' That's the way Roy was."

In Natchez, Mississippi, in the mid-1930s, a black murderer named Phil Williams was executed by the state for killing his wife and father-in-law. Contrary to custom Williams refused to repent, ask forgiveness, or address the Lord. He simply requested chicken dumplings and cigars for his last meal and went to the gallows without apology or remorse. It was an act that infuriated the white establishment but secretly pleased some of the blacks, who saw it as a rare act of defiance. Three sociologists in Natchez around the time of the execution interviewed a black man who explained Williams this way: "He wasn't much good at livin', but he knew how to die."

That would have been a good description of Roy, except that he wasn't dead yet. By his midtwenties Smith had served time in one of the worst prisons in the country, had been fired from innumerable jobs, had no steady line of work or steady relationship, didn't own property, didn't even own a car, and had a predilection for barroom fighting and petty theft that suggested at least a minor drinking problem if not outright alcoholism. Going back to Oxford was clearly not a good plan, and it was only a matter of time before he got himself into real trouble in Chicago. It was a measure of his situation that he decided his best option was to reenlist in the military—this time, the army. Even that didn't go well; barely a year into his service Roy was dishonorably discharged for what his prison records described as a "fraudulent enlistment." Other documents recorded that he had gone AWOL, noting that he was also hospitalized in Jacksonville, Florida, with a broken jaw. It was not hard to imagine that alcohol, the broken jaw, and the AWOL charge were somehow all connected on a long bad night in the bars of Jacksonville.

Roy Smith was not one of those people who left much paper behind him; leases, electric bills, car notes are invariably in someone else's name. The one thing he did show up regularly on, though, was police reports. If Roy Smith was anywhere for any length of time, the police seemed to know about it. Smith took his discharge in New Jersey in January 1955, and before the month was out he got into trouble across the river in New York. He was living in Harlem and working as a deliveryman for the Bailey Green Button and Buckle Company, and on January 29 he was arrested for trying to kill a woman with a pistol.

According to his arrest file, Roy had been drinking with three friends in a Harlem apartment when he started to get out of control. His friends pushed him out of the apartment and locked the door, which prompted Roy to pull a pistol out of his pocket and empty several rounds into the door. The gun was a Smith and Wesson .32-caliber "Victoria" that he bought for three dollars from a friend. Failing to shoot his way back into the apartment, he went down to the street and walked about a block, until he arrived at a shoe store at what was then 2031 Seventh Avenue. The time was ten minutes to seven. There was only one person in the store, a woman named Sally Wright, and Roy pulled the revolver out of his pocket and asked if she knew what it was.

In fact Sally Wright did *not* know what it was—the gun was so small she thought it was a toy. Smith allegedly pulled the trigger, but the pistol failed to fire, whereupon Smith slapped her across the face and continued pulling the trigger. Wright could hear the mechanism going *click, click, click.* Wright rushed to the window to wave for help, but she couldn't get anyone's attention, so she told Roy that she was going to go in back to get her dog. Unable to get the gun to fire and probably too drunk to keep Sally Wright from getting her dog—if indeed she even had one—Roy fled out the front door and walked several blocks home to his apartment in West 122nd Street.

He must finally have gotten the gun to work, because police responded to a report of shots fired in the hallway of the building, and Roy was arrested outside his apartment with the gun in his right-hand coat pocket. He was taken back to the Twenty-eighth

Precinct House in Harlem, where he was booked for illegal possession of a weapon, carrying a concealed weapon and first- and second-degree assault. Roy admitted to firing shots into his friends' apartment—an indiscretion that he attributed to too much alcohol—but he denied any involvement in the assault at the shoe store. Sally Wright positively identified Smith, however, and a ballistics expert found one live round in his revolver that had been dented by the gun's firing mechanism. Someone tried to fire that round, in other words, but it failed to go off. Bullets recovered from the apartment door were also examined, and a handwritten sentence at the bottom of the arrest file notes, "Ballistics supposed to have reported that [the bullets] were fired from defendant's gun."

On the face of it, if one believes the arrest report, Roy tried to kill someone and was prevented only by bad ammunition in a cheap gun. By all rights Sally Wright should have been dead with a bullet hole in her forehead. There were some odd things about the crime, though. First of all there was no explanation—and no legal reason—for why Roy was not charged with attempted murder. He put a gun to a woman's head and pulled the trigger; the fact that it didn't fire had no bearing whatsoever on his intention to take a human life. Second, there was no explanation for why the ballistics results were added to the crime report in longhand and couched in such uncertain terms. (Eight years later Roy's criminal records in Massachusetts stated, inexplicably, that the gun he used in the New York assault was made of wood.)

To confuse matters still further, Roy told police that he had two children and a wife named Dorothy, and that he had served in the army continuously since 1947. Both were straight-out lies and probably just an attempt to elicit the sympathy of the court; they didn't. Roy pleaded guilty to second-degree assault, and the Court of General Sessions sentenced Roy to one-to-six years in Sing Sing. He served almost his full sentence before being released on parole and returning to his apartment and his old job at Bailey Green. He managed to avoid the attention of the authorities for almost a year before surfacing in Boston, where he had been thrown into the Billerica House of Corrections for ten days for "threatening" behavior. Now Roy was living in Roxbury—Boston's version of Harlem—and working a variety of jobs, including as a cleaning man in a candy store and as a "lube man" at an auto shop. He was making sixty-five dollars a week and living from apartment to apartment, possibly because his utilities and back rent kept catching up with him.

He was also starting to show up more and more frequently on police blotters, though some of the crimes—a 1958 arrest for adultery that could have gotten him three years in prison—more reflected the times than the man. The adultery charge cost him only twenty-five dollars, but still, Roy Smith was clearly a man not fully in control of his life. Shortly after the adultery incident, Roy was arrested for assaulting someone with a bottle opener. The charges were eventually dropped, but his troubles didn't end there. Over the next few years he was charged with public drunkenness, for not being properly licensed to drive, for not properly registering his car, for attaching his plates to another car, for driving without car insurance, for driving under the influence, for driving with a suspended license—twice—for driving away from an accident, and again for public drunkenness. It was during this era of petty crime and bad judgment that Roy met a young black woman named Carol Bell and got her pregnant.

Carol Bell was from Plainfield, New Jersey, and worked for the Plymouth Coat Company in Boston. In Roy's arrest file she was described as his "paramour." Carol Bell was twenty-six years old and very pretty and had never had a child before. The young couple moved into a small apartment near Central Square, Cambridge, and in late November 1959, Carol gave birth to a son named Thomas. His nickname would be Scooter. What might have introduced a new era of stability and responsibility in Roy's life instead seemed just to have opened up another arena for legal trouble. Not even a year after his son's birth, Roy was picked up for "illegitimacy." At the time of his arrest, illegitimacy was defined as having a child out of wedlock, and it was a crime that only men could be charged with. There was a provision of the law, though, that required the man to provide financially for the mother of his illegitimate child, and it was under that provision that Roy was charged and put on probation. He managed to make it for about six months before getting picked up again for the same crime, and this time the courts got serious. Roy was sentenced to one year in Billerica prison.

By now Roy had been in the system so many times that the judges, the bailiffs, the prison guards must have started to recognize him. It is hard to know what to make of someone who sabotaged himself so expertly and regularly. The assault in New York aside— and the police report is sufficiently puzzling that it's ultimately unclear what really happened that night—Roy was not a habitually violent man, and he was certainly no career criminal. These were not calculated crimes, like robbery; these were crimes of convenience, committed by someone who couldn't afford to register and insure his car but still wanted to drive. These were the crimes of someone who was so chronically broke that he had to shortcut the system, but he did it so sloppily that he kept getting caught. Each arrest cost him money, which put him even farther behind than he was before. Roy was in an awful ratchet mechanism that seemed only to click downward.

It is not hard to see a drinking problem in Roy's endless situations, but there was more to it than that. Roy was different from Carol and most of his other friends in that he was from the South. He was from a part of the country where a black man driving a nice car was automatically pulled over because every sheriff in Mississippi knew there was no way he could've earned that kind of money legally, and they were probably right. The North was supposed to be different, and in some ways it was—you couldn't get lynched, for example—but you could still work your whole life and die almost as badly off as when you started. So why even try? Why even embark on the whole wretched enterprise?

No reason to, Roy must have decided early on—judging, at least, by the results. No life, it seems, could get driven downward that fast by bad luck alone.

TEN

BILL HAGMAIER, FORMER director of the National Center for the Analysis of Violent Crime:

"The classic serial killer is a true predator that sits and plans and fantasizes and even goes out and rehearses sometimes. When a serial killer is evolving, sometimes his first murder is almost an accident, or an act of violence that is really a displaced aggression; he's mad at someone else or something else and he kills and then says, 'Oh no, what have I done?' After a while he gets away with it, he feels comfortable, and he starts to rationalize: 'That person deserved it. I shouldn't have done it, but it was their fault, not mine.' And then he gets into a thing where the motivation is no longer sex or frustration—though that's part of it—the real motivation is *control*. He plays God. And he's not just playing God with the victims, he's playing God with the newspaper reporters, the police officers, the author who's going to come along later."

The National Center for the Analysis of Violent Crime is a department within the FBI that is devoted to understanding the mind of the serial killer. One of its founders was a former FBI agent named Robert Ressler, who conducted prison interviews with numerous multiple murderers to understand what drove them to kill. Ressler used the term "serial killer" to describe sexually sadistic murderers who did not seem to be able to stop killing. Whoever was strangling older women in Boston in the summer of 1962, he fit the profile of a classic serial killer almost perfectly. Furthermore he was almost certainly an "organized" killer, meaning that he was in control of his actions. Disorganized killers are often paranoid schizophrenics who have trouble distinguishing reality from fantasy—people who kill because voices command them to, for example, or because an outside force threatens to destroy them, and so they strike first. These people are not choosing to kill so much as—at least in their own minds—trying to survive. Because disorganized killers are often afflicted with full-blown psychosis, they tend to live alone or with their parents and have difficulty passing for "normal" in society. They pick their victims more randomly, often from their own neighborhood or social group, and leave behind crime scenes that, as Ressler says, "display the confusion of the killer's mind."

If the most terrifying thing about disorganized killers is that they're criminally insane, the most terrifying thing about organized killers is that they're *not*. This is how serial killer Ted Bundy described the moment of death: "You feel the last bit of breath leaving their body. You're looking into their eyes . . . a person in that situation is *God*. You then possess them and they shall forever be a part of you. And the grounds where you kill them or leave them become sacred to you, and you will always be drawn back to them."

Those words are clearly not the product of a disorderly mind; they are the product of a superbly articulate person who has spent a lot of time thinking about what it feels like to take a human life.

Ted Bundy admitted to killing thirty women and hinted that he may have killed three or four times that number. If one could design a machine for murdering young women, it would look a lot like Ted Bundy. He was classically good-looking, clean-cut, well educated—in psychology and law—and very, very angry. It was an anger that seemed to have been there since his childhood, when he was caught with a steak knife climbing into bed with his aunt. Most sexual predators choose highly vulnerable women as their prey—young girls, older women, prostitutes—but in his arrogance, Bundy did the opposite. He preyed on the smartest, most attractive women he could find, reveling in the fact that he could get them to trust him enough to allow him to kill them.

Bundy's description of what it felt like for him to choke a woman to death occurred during one of his many interviews with Special Agent Hagmaier, shortly before Bundy was executed by the state of Florida in 1989. Bundy had grown close to Hagmaier over the course of their interviews, and even requested that Hagmaier be present at his execution. He told Hagmaier toward the end that he could have avoided the death penalty if he'd gone along with his lawyers in an insanity defense. "I'm not crazy—you know I'm not crazy," Bundy said. "My ego killed me. If I'd pretended to be crazy like the psychiatrists and lawyers wanted me to be, I'd still be alive."

That distinction is the crux of a debate in the justice system. One could argue that anyone who tortures and kills human beings for sexual gratification is by definition insane, so any attempt to prosecute them must ultimately result in a verdict of not guilty by reason of insanity. The legal definition of an "insane" act, however, rests on a concept called the "irresistible impulse." A disorganized killer who is driven to kill and dismember young women because he believes he needs their blood to survive, for example, could reasonably be seen to be at the mercy of forces beyond his control—and therefore innocent. At some point, however, an irresistible impulse simply becomes an impulse that a person chooses not to resist, and that is when murderers become accountable for their actions.

Determining that point varies from state to state, but generally a person is legally accountable if he is both rational and understands that what he is doing is wrong. This is called the McNaughten rule, or the "policeman at the elbow" test. If the accused had a policeman standing next to him, the courts ask, would he still have committed the crime? A disorganized killer who murders with no stealth or planning and makes no attempt to hide evidence or conceal his identity might well commit murder whether a policeman is there or not. An organized killer, on the other hand, would refrain from killing because he would not want to get caught. Although organized killers are capable of the kind of butchery that characterizes a disorganized crime scene, their violence is not that of unrestrained savagery; rather it is a calm, sadistic process than can go on for days. Organized killers plan their murders in advance, assemble "murder kits" of implements that they'll need—knives, duct tape, handcuffs—and take great pains to cleanse the crime scene of evidence. As a result organized killers can go for years or decades without getting caught. They are engaged in a chess game not only with their victims but with the authorities, and it's a game they wouldn't be playing if they didn't think they would win.

An essential part of that game is sex. The predatory serial murder that lacks a component of sex—or more specifically, sexual sadism—has not yet been committed. That doesn't necessarily mean that the victim is raped; she might be sexually assaulted with an object or simply tied up, tortured, and killed in an elaborate scenario staged by the killer. But one way or another, sexual domination is the theme that runs through the great majority of the more highly choreographed murders. Typically a serial killer starts out by fantasizing murders based on pornography or detective magazines or his own private imaginings, and eventually "graduates" to acting these scenarios out with a victim. In that sense the victim is just a prop in the violent, highly sexualized fantasy life of the killer.

"I'm sorry to sound so cold about them," a serial killer and necrophiliac named Edmund Kemper said about his victims, "but to possess them the way I had to, I had to evict them from their bodies."

The National Center for the Analysis of Violent Crime identified 357 serial killers in the United States between the years 1960 and 1991. They are thought to have killed more than three thousand people, or roughly one person every three days. Because of a "dark figure" in serial killer statistics, though—murder victims who were never reported missing or whose bodies were never found—the number could be much higher. There are numerous theories for why some people start killing compulsively, but no single theory comes close to explaining the phenomenon adequately. Psychiatric disorders are obviously a tempting explanation, though it has been pointed out that getting away with murder is not particularly easy, and anyone who is too severely impaired is probably not going to remain free for very long. Severe sexual dysfunction afflicts many serial killers—some cannot achieve an erection with a living person, for example—but that simply begs the question of how that condition arose in the first place. There is one common element to many serial killers, however: suffering. Nearly half of all serial killers experienced physical or sexual abuse as children, and an even greater proportion were exposed to psychiatric problems, alcoholism and criminality in their family. Violence and sexual abuse are particularly effective at triggering the sort of reactions in children that are later expressed as sadism; the child withdraws into himself, pretending the abuse is actually happening to someone else, and eventually develops a deep capacity for fantasy and denial.

That fantasy life can then become the nucleus for a lifetime of violent sexual revenge.

THE MOTHER-HATE theory about the Boston Strangler that was popular for the first few murders abruptly stopped making sense at five thirty on the afternoon of December 5, 1962, when a young nurse named Audri Adams arrived home at her apartment on Huntington Avenue in Boston. Adams opened the double-locked door and saw one of her roommates, a twenty-one-year-old black woman named Sophie Clark, sprawled on the living room rug. Clark was a student at the Carnegie Institute of Medical Technology who had returned home early that afternoon to write a letter to her fiancé in New Jersey. She had three stockings twisted tightly around her neck and a gag forced into her mouth, and she lay exposed in the middle of the living room with her bathrobe fully opened and her legs spread apart. She had put up enough of a struggle for her glasses to be broken and her bra torn apart, and she had also been raped. Police investigators found a semen stain on the rug next to her.

The letter to her fiancé, who was supposed to visit a few days later, lay unfinished on a table. The letter mentioned that it was two thirty in the afternoon and that the weather was bad and that she was going to cook liver with onions and gravy and mashed potatoes for dinner. Apparently her young man hadn't written in a while, because Sophie also said that she hoped he wouldn't take that long to write again. The next sentence started with "I," and that was it. At some point after two thirty, she put down her pen and never picked it up.

Sophie Clark broke the pattern; she was young, she was black, she lived with other people, and she'd been raped. Psychologically the murder of a young woman presented a problem to police investigators: Why would a man driven by "mother-hate" suddenly kill and rape a young woman? Did he start out raping young women, graduate to killing older women, and then put the two crimes together? Or did he overcome some crippling insecurity with the older women that now allowed him to face sexually intimidating young women? Though psychologically tidy, that theory suffered the flaw that serial killers almost never change groups; if they start out killing children or old women or teenage boys, they rarely deviate. The alternative theory, of course, was that there were now two sexual predators in Boston. One focused his rage on older women but was psychologically—or physically—unable to rape them; the other probably started out raping young women and then was goaded by newspaper headlines into trying a killing of his own.

The Clark murder, however, did provide the police with one very strong clue. At two twenty that afternoon, another young black woman in the same building had heard a knock on her door and had opened it to a workman who said that he'd been sent to paint her apartment. The woman's name was Marcella Lulka; she told the man she knew nothing about it, but he just walked past her, did a quick tour of the apartment, and declared that her bathroom ceiling needed to be fixed. The man was medium height, powerfully built, and was wearing green pants and a black waist-length jacket.

You know, you have a beautiful figure, he said. Have you ever thought about modeling?

Marcella Lulka was alone in the apartment, and she knew she was in danger and that she had to think fast. She put her finger to her lips and told the man that her husband was sleeping in the next room. That was all that the stranger needed to hear; he mumbled an apology and ducked out of the apartment, and Marcella Lulka didn't think about him again until she heard police sirens.

Three weeks after Sophie Clark was killed, a twenty-three-year-old woman named Patricia Bissette was found dead in her Cambridge apartment by the superintendent of her building. She had been strangled by three stockings and a blouse and was lying in bed with her head turned to one side and the covers pulled up over her body. This was the first strangling victim to have been positioned in a discreet, peaceful way, a setting that police investigators refer to as "compassionate." Compassionate murder scenes are often the work of boyfriends and husbands who are filled with remorse after the initial outburst of violence. Bissette was nude except for her pajama top, which was pulled up to expose her breasts, and there was evidence that she had recently had sex. She had one boyfriend in Vermont and another who lived nearby, and the medical examiner soon determined that she was one month pregnant.

Initial news reports declared that Bissette's murder was not one of the "Boston Stranglings" because of the likelihood that one of her boyfriends had killed her. Neither man could be convincingly linked to the crime, however, which once again left authorities looking for someone who had knocked on a woman's door, been allowed in, and then killed her. After Patricia Bissette there was a lull in the murders until March 9, 1963, when sixty-eight-year-old Mary Brown was found beaten to death in a town north of Boston. The killer had crushed her head with a length of pipe, jammed a fork into one of her breasts, and raped her as she lay dying. The murder was so savage that it did not seem to fit the pattern of the other killings, though the public didn't have to wait long for one that did.

Two days later Israel Goldberg, rushing through his strangely quiet house, finally glanced into the living room and noticed something that looked like his wife's feet.

THE
TRIAL

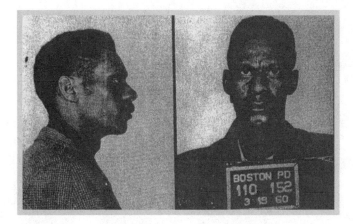

ELEVEN

A T 9:37 ON the morning of November 7, 1963, Roy Smith rose from his seat at the calling of his name and faced Judge Charles Bolster in a courtroom at the Middlesex Superior Court in East Cambridge. Smith stood in a prisoner's dock that came up to his waist and had a small door that was locked behind him to symbolize that he was not free on bail. (That practice was eventually abandoned as too prejudicial. Defendants now sit at a table next to their attorneys.) The room had thirty-foot ceilings and tall arched windows and was possibly the most ornate piece of architecture Roy had ever stepped into. Next to Roy at the defendant's table was his young attorney, Beryl Cohen, and across the room on his left was a twelve-person jury plus two alternates, all men. Judge Bolster was a respected but undistinguished judge who was known to be unapologetically fair toward the defense despite being an archconservative in an extremely liberal state.

"Mr. Foreman, gentlemen of the jury, the case before you is the case of the Commonwealth versus Roy Smith," began Richard

Kelley, the prosecutor. "He is charged—and the Commonwealth shall prove—that on March 11, 1963, he robbed, raped, and murdered Mrs. Israel Goldberg, Bessie Goldberg, at 14 Scott Road, in Belmont."

Kelley then plunged into the cumbersome language of a formal indictment. When he was done, he went back and repeated the charges, this time describing in detail the circumstances of each crime. The language was dense and repetitive and did not shy away from the awful particulars of the crimes. "You will hear evidence," Kelley told the fourteen men of the jury, "that this defendant Roy Smith, in his attack upon Bessie Goldberg, threw her on the floor, pushed up her girdle and underclothing, tore off and tore apart her underpants, and forcibly and against her will had intercourse with her. Penetrated the body of Bessie Goldberg and completed the act of intercourse upon her by force and against her will."

Richard Kelley was a tall man with a full head of curly black hair and bright, piercing eyes. He spoke carefully and thoughtfully with the flat vowels and dropped r's of a slight Boston accent, and after fourteen years as a trial lawyer was fully at ease before the jury. "And then you will hear that this same Roy Smith, sitting here in the courtroom today, did attack her further," he continued. "He tore from the garter belt the top of her stocking, took off the stocking from her leg and with that stocking wound around her neck, twisted it tightly, and for a period of time, until massive hemorrhages appeared on the face of Bessie Goldberg and caused her death, and you will hear from the medical testimony that her death was the result of that strangulation by Roy Smith, which will be described as a ligature. And that this Roy Smith, who sits before you today, was the one who for a period of time caused the life to gradually eke out of Bessie Goldberg and cause her death."

Kelley went on to explain to the jury that they would be hearing from many witnesses, all of whom had "their own capacity to observe and recall and their own manner of speech." The accounts of these people, he explained, would effectively become a mosaic that depicted the events of March 11, 1963. At times Kelley's account had the timeless quality of a fairy tale. "There was living at Belmont Mr. and Mrs. Israel Goldberg," he said. "They lived for some ten years at 14 Scott Road; that Mrs. Goldberg was a loving and devoted wife and a mother of a daughter who was quite grown up. That Mr. Goldberg got up at 7 o'clock that morning, had some conversation with his wife, left fifteen dollars by the night table and went downstairs, had his breakfast and did various things, leaving the house approximately at 9 o'clock."

Kelley's speech slowly gathered the force of true conviction. "You will hear that Roy Smith lied to police as to when he went to Belmont!" he promised. "When he left Belmont! What he was paid at Belmont! About what he did at Belmont! You will hear evidence of the weather that day. You will hear from the engineer who made the plans and you will hear other facts, Mr. Foreman and members of the jury, that I have not expressed to you at this particular time that will prove beyond a reasonable doubt each element in the three indictments against Roy Smith for the charges of rape, murder and robbery."

And so began the trial of Roy Smith, Negro, age thirty-five or thirty-six, charged with rape, robbery, and murder in the first degree.

THE MOST SERIOUS charge against Smith was, of course, the murder, which in Massachusetts carried with it an automatic death penalty if accompanied by a rape conviction. Murder is a category of homicide, which is a legally neutral term that simply means the killing of a human being. Suicide is technically a homicide, as are state executions and traffic fatalities. Centuries ago English common law, on which American law is based, developed the principal of "criminal" homicide. Criminal homicide was the unjustified killing of a human being by another human being and was punishable by death in all circumstances; if you killed you were killed in turn, end of discussion.

As concepts of fairness took hold in English society, criminal homicide was further divided into murder—which was, roughly speaking, a deliberate crime—and manslaughter, which was not. The manslaughter charge acknowledged that the world was an inherently chaotic and messy place and tried to avoid piling tragedy upon tragedy by allowing some leniency for people who did not set out to take a human life. Even that, however, was too blunt an instrument to sort out the various tragedies that man inflicts on man. If you throw a flowerpot out a window and kill someone on the street below, that may or may not be murder, depending on whether you were aiming. But suppose the pot slips out of your hands because you were drunk—is that a crime? If a man finds his wife in bed with another man and kills both in a blind rage, is he a murderer or simply a victim of circumstance? If he's a victim of circumstance, then would the man in the bed also be a victim of circumstance if he managed to kill the attacking husband instead?

There are no perfectly just answers to those questions, but early English law did understand the need to distinguish between different degrees of choice on the part of the killer. A person who kills deliberately but in a situation he did not construct—the enraged husband, for example—is guilty of voluntary manslaughter; the drunk who lets go of the flowerpot is guilty of involuntary manslaughter. Neither of those charges describes someone who intentionally sets out to kill another human being; that is reserved for the term "murder." The modern murder charge claims to know the mind of the killer, and claims to know that he or she acted with something called "malice aforethought." A man who kills with malice aforethought kills intentionally after contemplating his actions and discarding the idea of *not* killing. In Massachusetts malice aforethought also includes doing anything—like throwing a hand grenade into a crowded restaurant—that is likely to cause serious injury or death. In this sense, the word "malice" does not refer to spite or hatred on the part of the killer; "malice" refers to the fact that the killer had intentionality. It refers to the fact that at *some* point—years before the murder, or seconds—the person thought about killing another person and then carried it out.

The very pinnacle of the homicide pyramid—the very worst crime a person can commit, the only crime that regularly rates the death penalty—is murder in the first degree. Under most state statutes, murder in the first degree is defined as murder that is premeditated and deliberate. Like "malice," the term "premeditated" means that the idea of killing entered the mind of the killer beforehand, and the term "deliberate" means that the killer went on to weigh its merits and ultimately decided it was a good thing to do. The murder was committed with "cool purpose," rather than with "hot blood"; it was a conscious, rational decision by someone who did not value human life. And that was the crime Roy Smith was charged with committing.

According to his indictment, Smith showed intentionality by using a stocking to strangle Bessie Goldberg. Even without that element, however, first-degree murder can also be achieved by showing "extreme atrocity or cruelty," which is arguably true of a strangling, or by killing during the commission of another felony. And Roy Smith was charged not only with killing Bessie Goldberg but with raping and robbing her as well. Roy Smith, in other words, qualified for first-degree murder ten ways from Sunday.

Still, the U.S. Constitution guarantees due process to anyone charged with a crime, and that means that everyone who is arrested is presumed to be innocent until found otherwise by a jury. Referring to the country's collective sacrifice during the American Revolution, a Massachusetts judge wrote that it was "inconceivable that the people who depleted their resources in a long and bloody war to maintain their rights as freemen should have intended to deprive their citizens of an impartial trial before an unprejudicial jury." That meant that around nine o'clock on the morning of November 7, 1963, Roy Smith walked—unshackled—into Massachusetts Superior Court and took a seat in the defendant's box. For the next three weeks Roy Smith would watch a Middlesex County prosecutor try to convince a jury that had been *ordered* by the judge to presume his innocence that he was in fact guilty.

The prosecution, therefore, labored under the implacably humane ideal that, as later expressed in a Supreme Court decision, "it is better that ten guilty persons escape than that one innocent suffer." This is called the ten-to-one rule and can be traced through English common law all the way back to the Romans. The scales of justice—in theory, at least—are so heavily tilted in favor of the accused because it is thought that vastly more social harm results from jailing the innocent than from freeing the guilty. The reason that laws exist in the first place is to prevent social harm; so by definition those laws cannot cause more harm than the crimes they are meant to prevent.

In order to minimize that risk, Richard Kelley, as head prosecutor, bore something called the burden of production, which meant that he had to produce for the jury all evidence against Roy Smith; and the burden of persuasion, which meant that he had to assemble that evidence in a way that showed Roy Smith's guilt beyond a reasonable doubt. It was up to Judge Bolster to decide if Kelley had presented enough evidence for the case to go to a jury, and it was then up to the jury to decide whether that evidence showed that Smith was guilty. Once a jury has found someone innocent of a charge, they are innocent of it forever; a defendant could deliver a full confession to the police after his acquittal and still never be retried for the crime.

Furthermore Kelley had to prove not only that Roy Smith had killed Bessie Goldberg but that he had intended to, and that he had been in a criminal state of mind while he was doing it. In the United States one cannot be punished for merely thinking about something, and one cannot be punished for doing something without an accompanying criminal thought. You can fantasize all you want about committing murder, you can go out and buy a gun, you can draw a bead on someone from your attic window, but until you pull the trigger you have not committed a crime. There is no crime without an act—without, in fact, some kind of muscular contraction. On the other hand, if you trip while carrying a gun and accidentally shoot someone, you cannot be charged with first-degree murder because malice did not accompany the act. As Supreme Court justice Oliver Wendell Holmes, Jr., observed about criminal intent, "Even a dog distinguishes between being stumbled over and being kicked."

Roy Smith, on the other hand, was required to do absolutely nothing in his defense. He did not have to testify on his own behalf.

His attorney did not have to present other witnesses. His attorney did not have to present evidence. His attorney did not have to make an opening statement or cross-examine the state's witnesses. Theoretically, at least, Smith and his attorney could remain absolutely mute until the closing arguments without any adverse affect on the jury's verdict. The case was Kelley's to make or fail on the merits of his own evidence, and the jury was instructed by Judge Bolster not to draw any inference whatsoever from the manner of Roy Smith's defense.

Not only that, they were also instructed not to draw any conclusions from the fact that he had been arrested in the first place, that he had been held on bail, that he had been indicted by a grand jury or that he currently sat before them in the dock. Absolutely nothing that had happened up until this point—and nothing that the prosecutor said at any point in the trial—could be considered evidence against Roy Smith. Smith was a blank slate; he was exactly the sort of blank slate that the jurors themselves would wish to be if the roles were ever reversed, and they found themselves in the dock instead of him.

PROSECUTOR KELLEY HAD a case on his hands that was both utterly straightforward and oddly elusive. On the one hand, Smith was a longtime petty criminal with several assault charges on his record who was the last known person to have seen the murder victim alive, and who had left the victim's home less than an hour before the body was found. On the other hand, not one shred of physical evidence linked Smith to the body, and not one person saw him do anything wrong. People saw him go into the Goldberg home. People saw him leave the Goldberg home. People saw him take the bus, buy his liquor, ride around town, do whatever he did, but *no one* saw him kill Bessie Goldberg. What happened at 14 Scott Road that afternoon could never be determined with absolute certainty, so a jury of peers was required to decide what they thought happened. This was exactly the kind of case that the great, awkward loops of logic employed by the law are designed to resolve. Roy Smith's case was entirely circumstantial but nearly airtight, marred only by the fact that he refused to admit that he did it. A jury would have to step in and say it for him.

The commonwealth called an enormous number of witnesses to the stand. They called every single person who had shown up at Dorothy Hunt's apartment that night, including her nine-year-old daughter, Barbara Jean. They called the driver of the bus that Smith took back from Belmont. They called the clerk he bought liquor from; the pharmacist he bought cigarettes from; the pharmacist's other customer, who watched the transaction; and the milkman who dropped milk off at the Goldbergs' house. They called the cops who responded to the emergency call, the medical examiner who pronounced Bessie Goldberg dead, the doctor who examined her body and testified that she had been raped, and the woman who dispatched Smith to the cleaning job. They called every child playing on Scott Road that day, they called Israel and Leah Goldberg, and they called a fingerprint expert who testified, among other things, that one of the police officers had managed to leave his fingerprints at the crime scene.

The commonwealth, in fact, called so many witnesses—almost fifty—that all of Smith's acquaintances were taken. Cross-examination, when an attorney has the chance to ask questions of a hostile witness, has been described as the "greatest legal engine ever invented for the discovery of the truth." An attorney conducting a cross-examination has four basic options: He can challenge the credibility of the witness; he can show that the witness made an honest mistake; he can spin damaging testimony in his client's favor; or he can ignore the testimony entirely. One of the strengths of cross-examination is that it is inherently adversarial, but many of the state's witnesses knew Roy Smith, so Beryl Cohen would not necessarily want to become adversarial with these people.

What he could do, however—and the prosecution couldn't— was ask leading questions. A leading question is a question whose answer is suggested in its phrasing: "Is it not true, Mr. Goldberg, that you arrived home around four o'clock in the afternoon?" A good trial lawyer asks leading questions he already knows the answer to. A good trial lawyer asks leading questions that result in a long series of "yes" answers from the witness. A good trial lawyer strings these "yes" answers together into an interpretation of events that show his client to be innocent. In the hands of a good trial lawyer, a hostile witness simply becomes a conduit for the defense to offer its version of events to the jury.

The fingerprint man was the first witness of real consequence, and the first one who perhaps raised a flicker of doubt in the minds of the jury. He was a state police officer named Arthur Morrison who led the jury through a tortuous explanation of the science of fingerprint analysis and concluded that Roy Smith had, in fact, been in the Goldberg house that day. Moreover, Smith had at some point touched a mirror above the mantelpiece near where Bessie Goldberg's body was found.

This would have been devastating testimony in a trial where the accused had denied having been at the murder scene, but that was not the case. Smith had readily admitted to having been at the Goldberg home, so the great lengths to which the commonwealth went to prove his presence were in some sense wasted effort. Under cross-examination Beryl Cohen coaxed from Officer Morrison the fact that not only had another police officer contaminated the scene with his own prints, but that Roy Smith's prints had appeared neither on Bessie Goldberg's handbag nor on her jewelry box. That seemed odd, considering that the primary motivation for the murder was alleged to be robbery. Furthermore Officer Morrison hadn't thought to dust the front and back doorknobs for prints, which might have shown whether Smith had let himself out of the house or not. Smith told the Belmont police that Bessie had shown him out at the end of the day; one palm print on a doorknob would virtually have sealed his fate.

Lacking incontrovertible evidence or damning testimony, a trial inevitably turns into a popularity contest, and this one was no exception. You cannot be found guilty for who you are, only for what you have done, but who you are unavoidably affects what the jury thinks you are capable of doing. Roy Smith was not going to take the stand in his own defense because, under the laws of the day, that would make him open to questioning from Richard Kelley about his criminal record, and Kelley would certainly bring up his occasional capacity for violence. Not only was it an all-male jury, it was an all-white jury—the result not of racism but of the fact that jurors were drawn from voter lists—and the idea of a black ex-con running amok in the suburbs would be an idea that these jurors would find deeply disturbing.

So Roy Smith would not testify; Roy Smith would sit idly in the dock in the suit he'd bought for the occasion watching a roomful of white people argue over his fate. If Kelley could not bring out Smith's terrible past, though, he *could* bring out his somewhat shabby present. The first chance he had to do that was with Dorothy

Martin, who assigned temporary jobs at the Division of Employment Security and had sent Roy Smith out to Belmont on the morning of March 11. "Would you tell the jury," Kelley asked her, "what you said, what he said and what was done at that time?"

"I asked him why he hadn't come earlier," Mrs. Martin said. "And he told me he went to another customer's house, but she wasn't home. I am always detecting odors, so I asked him if he had been drinking. He said no, so I leaned a little forward and he leaned a little backwards. And I said, 'You know, we wouldn't send anyone out who's been drinking.' He said he hadn't, so I sent him out."

The incident stuck in Mrs. Martin's mind, and around four o'clock that afternoon she picked up the phone to call the Goldberg house. She wanted to know how Roy had worked out, and she also had another job to give him. Just as she was reaching for the phone, it rang. It was a police officer, though he didn't identify himself as such. He just asked Mrs. Martin if she had sent a man out to the Goldbergs' to do some cleaning. Mrs. Martin said that she had, and went on to ask if she should send Smith on other jobs.

I don't know, the man said and hung up. Puzzled, Mrs. Martin called back, but no one answered. She checked the line with the operator and kept calling until eventually Israel Goldberg answered.

Richard Kelley: "Now when you spoke to Mr. Goldberg late in the afternoon of March 11, 1963, could you describe to the jury the manner of his speech?"

Mrs. Martin: "He was highly excited, emotional, and I identified myself and asked him was Roy Smith there. He said, 'Who is that man you sent out?' He said, 'She's dead!' I didn't get it, and he said again, 'She's dead!' He screamed and said, 'He killed her!'"

Mrs. Martin said that at that point she started screaming as well.

Soon after Mrs. Martin stepped down, Richard Kelley called

Israel Goldberg himself to the stand. If Roy Smith, in the minds of some, might have seemed a likely murderer, Israel Goldberg must have looked exactly the opposite: a short elderly Jewish man who, according to testimony, wore a fedora and overcoat in cold weather and was careful not to step off the pavement when it snowed, so as to keep his shoes dry. Richard Kelley waited for Mr. Goldberg to settle himself on the stand and then led him, question by question, through the last day of his wife's life.

Kelley took him through his workday in Chelsea, where Goldberg ran a small office building that he had inherited from his father. Kelley took him home at the end of the day down Route 60, stopping for twelve minutes at O'Brien's Market, in Medford, to buy frozen peas and frozen orange juice and frozen succotash and frozen string beans, French-style. It must have been unspeakably painful for Israel Goldberg to recall this day in sufficient detail to convict the man accused of murdering his wife, but Kelley did not let up on him. Kelley made Mr. Goldberg park in his driveway and climb out of his car and take the packages of frozen food in his arms. Kelley made Mr. Goldberg say hello to the children playing kickball in the street and walk up to the front door and put his keys in the lock. Kelley made Mr. Goldberg open the door and step into his house and then walk into the kitchen and start putting his purchases away.

Mr. Goldberg had seen something, though—he'd seen something on his way in. Out of the corner of his eye, Mr. Goldberg explained, he'd noticed that the hose of the vacuum cleaner was on the floor in the living room and that the furniture was out of place. He hadn't thought much about it because it simply meant the house was being cleaned, which was as it should be, but something was wrong. If the house was being cleaned, Israel Goldberg thought as he unloaded his frozen vegetables, then why was it so quiet? And if the house was done being cleaned . . . why was the vacuum cleaner still out?

"I ran into the bedroom," Israel Goldberg told the court. "I dropped my overcoat at the foot of the stairs. And I was hollering."

Kelley: "What were you saying?"

"*Bess! Bess! Bess!*' And I walked into the living room and I had gone in four or five steps and I noticed my wife's feet. I thought she had fainted and I didn't know what to do but I rushed to her and then I noticed—"

Kelley: "You saw what?"

"Just her panties showing, up to her waist. I didn't know what to do, I noticed her mouth, a tilt—there was a slight tilt and her mother had had a shock, and I thought she'd had a shock and it seemed puffed, a slight tilt, a puff, I think. I just stood there and then I noticed—I had never seen my wife wearing a scarf and she had—it looked like a beige or brown flimsy material around her neck a big bow. And I was wondering why she was wearing it."

In fact Israel Goldberg was looking at the stocking that had been used to strangle his wife. "What did you do then, sir?" Kelley asked.

"I waited a second, trying to figure it out," said Israel Goldberg. "And I didn't know what to do. I ran to the kitchen. And I telephoned the police."

TWELVE

ROY GOT OUT of Billerica for the second time in September 1962, and almost immediately he and Carol decided to move out of their Cambridge apartment to a bigger one in Boston. Shortly before they moved, a friend named Dorothy Hunt stopped by to see if she might move into the apartment that Roy and Carol were vacating on Marvin Place. Dorothy was a black woman from the Deep South who was raising two little girls on a teacher's salary and living in essentially slumlord housing a few blocks away. She and Roy had met when he moved to Boston, and they had lived with or near each other ever since. Roy had become particularly close Dorothy's younger daughter, Barbara Jean, calling her "Little Sister," because she shared a name with his own younger sister. He carried a photograph of her in his wallet and eventually asked Dorothy if he could be her godfather.

"He was a southerner and I'm a southerner—I'm from Gastonia, North Carolina," says Dorothy Hunt, now in her living room in a second-floor apartment in the town of Somerville. She is soft-spoken and dignified in the way that old people who have outlived a lot of bad history often are. "Sometimes the southerners would get together, you know—that southern hospitality. If you overstayed you could sleep over, no big thing. My mother told me, 'You never turn anybody away. Don't turn anybody away at night because anything can happen to them . . . wait till the daytime so they can see their way.'"

Dorothy wound up living briefly on Marvin Place before moving to a grim little flat-roofed building on Brookline Street. It had clapboard-style tin siding and a brick facade and shallow bay windows that her daughters could look out to see if any of the neighborhood children were playing on the street below. On the bottom floor was a tavern called the Brookline Café, and the other two floors had tenants. Around five o'clock on the afternoon of March 11, 1963, Roy Smith climbed the three flights to Dorothy's new apartment and found her in the kitchen cooking dinner. He had not seen her since she stopped by Marvin Place looking for a place to live. In her living room were two men Roy knew from his days in the neighborhood, Ronnie Walcott and Ronnie Clark. Walcott was black and Clark was white, and they were drinking buddies known on the Coast as "the Two Ronnies."

In the days after the murder, police investigators interviewed virtually every person who had contact with Roy Smith; as a result his movements on March 11 are known almost to the minute, and the conversations he had—and that others had about him—are recorded word for word. Sitting with Walcott and Clark was a young white woman named Peggy, who had arrived a few minutes before Roy. She baby-sat for Dorothy and was dating Ronnie Clark—"White Ronnie"—who happened to live nearby. Peggy had fled home at fifteen because her parents objected to her socializing with black boys, and since then she had given birth to a mixed-race child and, as a result, been committed to a state-run school for wayward girls. Now she was eighteen and living in and out of Dorothy's apartment until she got her feet on the ground. She was the youngest person there that night and the only one who did not drink.

By coincidence Peggy had noticed Roy Smith on the street several minutes earlier and remembered him when he walked in the door. They said hello to each other, and Roy went into the kitchen to talk to Dorothy. He had a half-pint of Schenley's whiskey and two quarts of beer with him, and he opened up the Schenley's and asked Dorothy if she'd seen his girlfriend recently. Roy said he hadn't heard from her in days and that the only way she could hurt him was by taking Scooter away. Dorothy told Roy she hadn't seen Carol in months, which was the truth, and went on to complain that her television had just stopped working. There was sound but no image, which wasn't keeping the Two Ronnies from listening to it as if it were a radio.

Roy offered to lend her a spare television that he had at his apartment in Boston. While they were discussing how to get over there, a black man named William Cartwright showed up. Roy had never met Cartwright before, but he put two dollars in his hand and asked him to run out and buy a half-pint of Old Grand-Dad. That was quickly polished off, and next time it was Roy who walked up Brookline Street to Boyer's Liquors and asked for another half-pint of Schenley's. It was the second half-pint he'd bought in the past hour; he gave the clerk two dollars and got forty-three cents back, and after he walked out, the clerk shook his head and said to the other man stocking liquor in the back, "If it was me I'd 'a bought a pint."

Roy went back to the apartment, and they all started in on the second Schenley's. Roy had been drinking for three hours, and Ronnie Clark had been drinking steadily all day, having started after breakfast. By eight o'clock they were out of whiskey again, and Roy headed out in search of more. Instead of going to Boyer's, he walked up Mass. Ave. and pulled open a heavy wood door on a low brick building and stepped into the smoky darkness of Dan Stack's Lunch.

Sitting at a booth in the back when Roy walked in was a black woman named Sadie, who noticed him but didn't realize she'd met him before. Something about him must have caught her eye, however. She watched him go to the bar and order a drink from a bartender named Sally Flaherty and then walk to the back and go to the men's room. Sadie lived in Boston and was married to a man who worked in a "whiskey store," as she called it, and she had been drinking since two in the afternoon. She had taken a taxi into Cambridge to see a friend of hers named Lucille Reid, and she and Reid had split a half-pint of Old Thompson before Sadie continued on to Dan Stack's. There she sat by herself and kept working away at the Old Tom until Roy showed up.

Dan Stack's was on the corner of Columbia and Mass., and Roy probably knew it from when he'd lived on Columbia Street several years earlier. If not, he knew it because it was legendary as one of several places in Central Square where blacks and whites drank together without too much trouble. Stack was no beacon of enlightenment, but he knew plenty of blacks and refused to discriminate against anyone who had money to pay for a drink. According to his sons, Stack had come over from Ireland by freighter at seventeen because he had killed a policeman who had come onto their property and shot his father's dogs. The family owned an old shotgun but was too poor to afford ammunition, so young Dan Stack poured borrowed gunpowder into a used paper cartridge and packed the rest with ball bearings from his bicycle wheels. He waited outside the policeman's house until the man returned from the pub and then shot him dead with his one homemade round.

Stack fled Ireland with his uncle and brother. The only port they could get free passage to—in exchange for years of labor in a Canadian mine—was Montreal, but they had no intention of working in a mine. As soon as they pulled into port they slipped the ship and started walking. They had the address of an Irish girl from a nearby farm who had found work as an au pair in Belmont, Massachusetts, and so they headed south. They slept in barns and ate at churches and walked out of Canada and down through Vermont and New Hampshire and arrived, starving and exhausted, on the girl's doorstep. This was during Prohibition, and it didn't take Stack long to capitalize on the odd notion of illegal drinking. He worked as a gravedigger and then as a bellhop and eventually bought a triple-decker in Somerville, tore out the second floor and built a three-hundred-gallon whiskey still. He started supplying moonshine to the Vendome Hotel, and when Congress ruined everything by legalizing drinking, he shut down the still and paid cash for a former A&P supermarket in Central Square. He called the place Dan Stack's Lunch, and it quickly became a neighborhood favorite.

Dan Stack served beer and whiskey straight or with soda or water, and if customers wanted anything more complicated, he put the bottles down on the bartop and told them to make it themselves. There were monstrous fights at the bar, arguments over politics or religion or women, and the accepted custom was that the man who was left standing had to buy the other guy a drink. Stack smoked three packs a day but seemed to be made of reinforced concrete with fists like three-pound hammers and a face as hard as a shovel. Well into his sixties he would handle problems at the bar by carefully taking off his glasses, taking out his hearing aid, and punching someone's lights out.

The bartop at Dan Stack's was mahogany and ran the length of the room under a high ceiling of stamped tin, painted white. Magnesium lights hung down on poles over two rows of wooden booths, and a jukebox scratched out music from a back wall. The evening of March 11 came in with a steady sleet, and the Irishmen must have been at the bar in their soaked wool overcoats with cigarettes between their teeth and shots of whiskey in front of them on the mahogany. Roy would have made his way cautiously through this crowd because it was filled with drunks, and he was drunk, and you never knew what was going to set someone off. He spotted Sadie at the back of the room and went up to her and introduced himself, and asked her the same thing he'd asked Dorothy, whether she'd seen his girlfriend.

Sadie said she hadn't. Sadie had known Dorothy for twenty years, and Roy invited her back to the apartment to continue drinking with them. They put on their coats and walked outside, stepping carefully in the slush, and got a taxi even though it was only a few blocks. Before climbing the stairs to Dorothy's, Roy ducked into Boyer's and bought another half-pint of Schenley's. For the third time he handed the clerk two dollars and got forty-three cents back. "I'd have bought a fifth," the cashier said to the other counterman after Roy left. Roy and Sadie made their way up to the third floor and knocked on the door. Dorothy and Billy Cartwright and the Two Ronnies and Peggy were there, most of them still drinking. A guy named Jimmy Dottin showed up soon after; Dottin was a welder from the Coast who lived in Roxbury and was godfather to one of Dorothy's girls. Roy had bought the evening edition of the

Record American when he was out at the bar, and he pulled it out of his overcoat pocket and dropped it on the table. Peggy picked it up to look at it, and Roy asked if she saw anything interesting.

It was a strange question, because Roy could hardly have bought the paper without noticing the inch-and-a-half headline on the front page that screamed, HOUSEWIFE STRANGLED IN BELMONT. Peggy said that there *was* some interesting news, and proceeded to read, "A 62 year-old Belmont woman, Mrs. Bessie Goldberg of 14 Scott Rd., in the exclusive Belmont Hill section, was found strangled yesterday in the living room of her home. Israel Goldberg, 65, arrived home shortly before 4 p.m. and found his wife prone in the living room of their luxurious home. A silk stocking was wound tightly around her neck. The victim is the ninth strangle victim in the Greater Boston Area."

If Roy Smith recognized Bessie Goldberg's name, he didn't show it. He either truly didn't recognize the name of the woman he'd just worked for, or he was faking it. If he was faking it, he was either guilty and didn't want to admit having been there that day, or he was innocent and was too horrified to cope with the implications. You're an unemployed black man from the South with a seventeen-year arrest record, and you work for a white lady who was found dead less than an hour later; the cops are *definitely* going to want to talk to you. It's hard to know what the "right" reaction would be in that situation. It's possible that there is none.

The conversation moved on from the murder to Sadie, who some in the apartment later claimed was almost too drunk to walk. Dorothy considered Sadie's husband a troublemaker and was worried that he would show up at her apartment, so she asked Roy to send her home. Roy and Jimmy Dottin walked Sadie out of the apartment and carried her down the stairs to the ground floor.

Sadie realized she had left her purse in the kitchen, so Roy ran back up and got it and then helped Jimmy walk Sadie up to Mass. Ave. and load her into a taxi. Roy walked alone back up Brookline Street and climbed the stairs one more time. The apartment didn't have much heat, so Dorothy blocked off most of the rooms and had everyone sit in her bedroom to listen to the broken television. The booze was finished and people were starting to doze off and after a couple of hours a decision was made to drive Billy Cartwright's car over to Boston to pick up Roy's spare television. Sometime around midnight Roy, Dorothy, Billy, and Ronnie Walcott put on their coats and went back down to the street.

Ronnie sat next to Billy up front, and Roy sat with Dorothy in the back. They took a right on Mass. Ave. and drove without speaking past the wastelands of Albany Street and the railroad tracks and then across the empty darkness of the Charles River. They passed through downtown Boston and across the deserted expanse of Huntington Avenue, and at Columbus, Roy told Billy to go right. The first left was Northampton, and Billy turned on that and continued slowly up the street. They crossed over Tremont Street, and around midblock Roy told Billy to slow down because they were at his building. Billy and Roy saw them at the same time: two men standing in the shadows across the street from Roy's apartment.

They're here, Roy said.

He told Billy to keep driving, and they continued down Northampton Street to Washington Street and stopped in front of the Highland Tap for one last round. Roy paid for it. When they were done they all got back in the car, and Billy circled back around Northampton one more time. He was just starting to slow down in front of number 175 when Roy spotted the two men again and told

Billy not to stop. They returned to Cambridge without the television, and Roy spent that night on a spare box spring in Dorothy's apartment.

The two men were cops, and they would be there all night waiting for Roy Smith to come home.

THIRTEEN

ATTORNEY BERYL COHEN stood around five feet eight and had a broad face and a full head of disorderly hair that made him look as if he might just have stepped off an overnight train. His style of speaking—of thinking, perhaps—was offhand to the point of seeming distracted. He talked as if he were simultaneously listening to a conversation in the next room and juggling three different things he wanted to say. It was a sophisticated style that could be very effective. "Mr. Goldberg," Beryl Cohen asked on the second morning of the trial, "in the photograph that you identified this morning, do you recall whether or not both shoes were on both feet?"

"No, sir."

"Now, when you first saw your wife's feet," Cohen went on, "did you move closer into the living room?"

"Yes, sir."

"Was there some furniture to get around?"

"I think so. I'm not sure."

"Did you push any furniture around to get in?"

"I doubt it."

"Why do you doubt it?"

"Because I don't remember touching anything."

One can imagine Cohen letting a moment or two pass to allow the supposed implications of this sink in with the jury. "Well, this business of touching anything," he went on. "You testified yesterday at great length to not having touched anything from the time you discovered your wife to the time the police came."

"I don't think I said it that way."

"Well, I'm sorry then."

"I didn't touch my wife."

"Then you observed her full body, is that correct?"

"Sooner or later, yes."

"Did you remain in a standing position, or did you kneel down?"

"For a moment, I am quite sure, I stooped. I—"

"You didn't bend your knees, or put your knees to the floor?"

"No, sir."

"Your vision was directed to the scarf around her neck. Did you attempt to loosen it at all?"

"I touched nothing, sir."

"Well, Mr. Goldberg, were you preserving the scene?"

"No, sir. What do you mean?"

"Mr. Goldberg, you don't understand what I mean by 'preserving the scene'?"

"I don't understand."

"Do you understand perjury? Mr. Goldberg, on March 9, 1917, you became an attorney-at-law, is that correct?"

"Yes, sir. Is that the date? Yes, sir."

"I will ask you again, Mr. Goldberg. Were you preserving the scene in the living room by not touching anything?"

"Probably that was in the back of my mind, I don't know. I know—one thing I know, it was helpless."

"You knew you were helpless?"

"To help, in the manner of helping. I saw no breathing."

"Now, you were two or three feet away?"

"Yes."

"You didn't touch her?"

"No, sir."

"Did you know that she was dead?"

"As far as being a doctor, no, but—I saw no movement."

"How long did you observe her before you left the living room?"

"Seconds."

"Seconds?"

"As far as I know," Israel Goldberg said, "it was seconds."

At the core of every criminal trial is the fact that almost anything can be presented in two different ways—otherwise there would be no judges in the world, no courts, no lawyers, no juries. Roy Smith leaves the Goldberg house around three o'clock and strolls across the street to buy a pack of cigarettes. A defense attorney would say that this reveals a clear conscience: No one would be stupid enough to murder a woman in Belmont and then linger any longer than necessary in the area. Nonsense, the prosecutor would counter; that's just the kind of cold-blooded son of a bitch Smith was: He raped a woman and then had to have a smoke.

To some degree every trial is an exercise in stretching reality as far as it will go; whoever has to stretch reality least in order to explain events wins. Had Israel Goldberg significantly altered the murder scene, Beryl Cohen would have claimed that the evidence was tainted. In fact he did not touch the murder scene at all, which allowed Cohen to say that he was intentionally preserving the scene—and, by implication, may have committed the murder himself. Either way Smith was a little closer to being exonerated. Cohen didn't have to prove that theory—he didn't even have to *believe* it—but he had to turn it into a reasonable possibility. If he succeeded in that and one juror couldn't get the idea out of his mind, the jury would be deadlocked and Smith would get a new trial. Ideally ten guilty men go free for every innocent man who gets locked up. That means that not only are there significant numbers of innocent people in prison, but that ten times that number of real criminals are set loose. Both ideas, in their way, are horrifying; Smith's fate depended in part on which one the jury found more horrifying.

Later in his cross-examination of Israel Goldberg, Cohen brought up a man named Harold Breaker, who worked at the gas station around the corner from the Goldberg house. Years earlier, Mr. Goldberg had taken to playing cribbage there several nights a week with other men in the neighborhood, though he stopped after his wife's murder. He still bought gas there, though, even though Mr. Breaker was going to be a witness at the trial. "When you'd be at Mr. Breaker's for these card games and conversations," Cohen asked Goldberg, "there had to have been several men there, is that correct?"

"Yes, sir."

"Do you ever recall a conversation about the Strangler?"

"No, sir, not that I remember, not in any specific—"

"You don't recall discussing the Boston Strangler, so-called?"

"No."

"Mr. Goldberg, sometime after March 11, did you attend the funeral of Beverly Samans?"

The murder of Beverly Samans was one of the bloodiest, and one of the most recent, of the Boston stranglings. "Yes, sir," answered Mr. Goldberg.

"She had been strangled in Cambridge, is that correct?"

"Yes, sir."

"Do you recall whether she had been strangled with a silk stocking?"

"I don't know what kind—probably a stocking."

"You attended her funeral?"

"Not the funeral, no—at the school they had a memorial service."

"For Beverly Samans?"

"Yes, sir."

"You didn't know her?"

"No, sir."

In some ways it was extraordinary that Goldberg was managing to address Cohen politely or even to answer him at all. Here was a man, after all, who was all but accusing him of killing his own wife; between different men in different circumstances, that conversation itself would have ended in violence. If, as a defense strategy, it was a distasteful one, that was because Cohen was blocked from knowing almost anything about the prosecution's case and so was unable to develop a plausible rebuttal. Under the laws at the time, pretrial discovery—where the prosecution is required to turn information over to the defense—was almost nonexistent. Today, if a prosecutor cuts a deal with one defendant in exchange for testimony against another, or if a crime lab turns up DNA evidence at a crime scene, the defense is entitled to know about it—the information is "discoverable." The idea behind pretrial discovery is that the court theoretically has no interest in convicting someone with evidence that cannot withstand the scrutiny of the defense. "You don't conduct trial by ambush," as one Massachusetts judge put it. "You don't play hide-the-ball."

In Massachusetts in 1963, however, pretrial discovery was strictly at the discretion of the court. So months before the trial, Beryl Cohen went before the court to request, among other things, that he be allowed to inspect the crime scene, that he be granted access to the autopsy and crime lab reports, that he be given a transcript of the grand jury minutes and of Roy Smith's interrogation in the Belmont police station, and that the prosecution provide the exact time and manner of Bessie Goldberg's death. "A trial in which a man's life is at stake should be more than a mere contest of wits," he had told Judge McCaulay, who presided over the pretrial hearing. "The fundamental purpose of a criminal trial is not solely to convict the accused. The truism should be recognized that 'The truth should have nothing to fear from the light.'"

By 1979 everything Cohen was asking for would have been granted automatically. It is thought that if the defense has access to every component of the prosecution's case and *still* can't rebut it, then an innocent man is almost certainly not going to prison. Cohen was allowed to inspect the crime scene accompanied by a Belmont police officer, he was allowed to inspect the autopsy report, and he was given something called a bill of particulars, which was supposed to set out the broad outlines of the commonwealth's case. All of Cohen's other motions were denied. As a result Cohen was less able to develop a rebuttal to the commonwealth's case and instead had to develop his own. Inevitably that would mean suggesting that Israel Goldberg could have committed the murder.

It would also mean suggesting that Roy Smith was primarily a suspect because of his race.

"MR. PIZZUTO."

"Yes."

"Do you recall the first time you learned what happened to Mrs. Goldberg?"

"Oh, I would say about five o'clock."

"Did you discuss it with a great many people?"

"No, I never discussed it with anybody."

"Never discussed what?"

"I didn't know nothing about the case, didn't discuss anything with anybody."

"There was no case then."

"Well, you are just saying that—"

"Just let me ask the questions. If my question is worded improperly you can tell me that and don't answer it."

Louis Pizzuto was one of the commonwealth's most important witnesses because he—and he alone—claimed that Roy Smith looked agitated and nervous as he walked away from the Goldberg home. Without Pizzuto, Smith was just another man walking down the street. Pizzuto was the man who owned a sub shop called Gigi's. Around three o'clock on the afternoon of March 11, he had seen Roy Smith walk past his shop on the opposite side of Pleasant Street. A black man was not a common sight in Belmont, so Pizzuto got up from his seat and walked to the doorway to follow Smith's progress. He watched Smith go into the pharmacy and then emerge a few minutes later and continue walking up Pleasant Street toward the bus stop. According to Pizzuto, Smith glanced behind him continually as he walked. Sometime later, Pizzuto left his shop and walked across the street to the pharmacy.

Pizzuto was a big man and as he testified he pulled a handkerchief out of his pocket and began to dab the sweat off his face.

"You asked the kid in the drug store," Beryl Cohen went on, "whether the colored fellow went in there?"

"Yes."

"Is that what you said to him? Did you say, 'Was there a colored fellow in there buying cigarettes?'"

"I said, 'Did a colored fellow come into the store?' I didn't ask him 'cigarettes.'"

"Did you say 'colored fellow'?"

"Yes."

"That was Kenneth Fitzpatrick you were talking to?"

"I don't know his name, he works in the drugstore."

"Did you say to Ken Fitzpatrick, 'Did you see the big darkie?'"

"No, I did not."

"You didn't say that?"

"I might have said 'negro.'"

"You might have said 'negro.' Did you say 'nigger'?"

"Well, I might have said 'nigger.'"

"You might have said 'nigger.' Did you say, 'the big darkie'?"

"I wouldn't say it."

"I'm asking you *whether* you said it."

"Well, yes, I think I said it."

"You did say it. What did you say?"

"'Was that nigger in your place.'"

"Did you say, 'Big nigger'?"

"No, I didn't say no 'big nigger.'"

Pizzuto had alerted the Belmont police that he'd seen a black man walking down Pleasant Street, but he'd alerted them *before* he knew there'd been a murder nearby; he'd alerted them simply on principal after noticing police cars in the area. Everyone on Pleasant Street, it seemed, had noticed Smith walk by, and perhaps everyone on Pleasant Street had had the same thought: What's that black guy doing out here? Not everyone, however, was as forthright about it as

Pizzuto. Belmont was a sophisticated town where few people would openly say anything racist, but that didn't mean they weren't thinking that way. The merchants in Belmont Center or the bankers up on the Hill might have been just as suspicious of Smith as Pizzuto was, but most would never have owned up to it.

The thing about racism, though, is that it doesn't necessarily mean that the black guy *didn't* do it, either. The commonwealth's case against Smith advanced across a broad front that kept Cohen dashing back and forth on the parapets like a man trying to defend a fortress by himself. First came the children. All four of them were asked by Kelley whether they understood what it meant to tell the truth, and all of them answered that they did. Three of the children testified that they passed Roy Smith on their way home around three o'clock and that he looked as if he was in a hurry but not necessarily nervous. The children all testified that soon after they got home they organized a kickball game in front of the Goldberg house, and that Dougie had scored eight runs in a row by the time Mr. Goldberg got home. They testified that while they were playing no one else came or went from the house until Mr. Goldberg arrived, and that he was only inside a few minutes before he rushed back out. Susan Faunce said that when he reemerged he was screaming and crying so hard that she could barely understand him. "Why did this happen to me? Oh, my Bessie!" she understood him to say.

"Maybe she went into town," Myrna Spector said to Mr. Goldberg, trying to be helpful. Moments later the children heard the sirens.

After the children came the issue of the money. Richard Kelley called a succession of taxi drivers, liquor store clerks, pharmacists, and Roy Smith's friends to add up exactly what Smith spent in the twenty-four hours following the murder. And the amount—"Not a grand total to you . . . but for Roy Smith, it was blood money," as Kelley would later tell the jury—was thirteen dollars and seventy-two cents. That was eight dollars more than he should have had, according to what Smith said he was paid at the Goldberg's. Even more damning, the liquor store clerk said that he'd seen Smith pull a ten and five ones out of his pocket when he paid for his liquor, and Israel Goldberg testified that he'd left a ten and five ones on his Bessie's night table before leaving that morning.

And then there was the rape. Why did Roy Smith—who was accused of killing Bessie Goldberg so that he could get away with the robbery—also rape her? At his feet was a dying sixty-two-year-old woman. Was he overcome by lust? By rage at whites? Was he simply insane? Kelley offered no psychological or legal theory on the rape, beyond the fact that Smith was possibly drunk and essentially capable of anything. That rape had occurred, however, was beyond dispute: Dr. Arthur McBey of the state police crime laboratory testified that a vaginal smear taken from Bessie Goldberg showed "numerous intact spermatozoa." The fact that the sperm cells were intact meant that the sex act had occurred very recently. This was not sex that had happened a day or a week earlier; this was sex that had happened at the same time as the murder. Furthermore there was a small stain on the outside of Smith's trousers that turned out to be sperm as well, though it could not be determined how old it was. But it looked very much as if Roy Smith had raped Bessie Goldberg and then just pulled up his pants and fled.

The final component of the commonwealth's case was the trip to Boston to pick up Smith's television set. Every person in the car that night testified in one way or another that Smith did not want to stop at the apartment when he saw that there were policemen outside it. Cartwright's testimony was particularly damning: "I got to

Shawmut, he asked me to slow down, then he said, 'Go faster, they're still here,'" he told Richard Kelley under direct examination. "I seen two gentlemen in the dark on the other side of the street."

This was crucial for the commonwealth. Other than Louis Pizzuto, no one who encountered Smith on the afternoon of the murder thought that he looked agitated. That was a problem. Murder upsets people; it even upsets murderers. Kelley had shown that Smith had opportunity to commit the crime and that he had too much money in his pocket; now with Cartwright he could show that Smith was avoiding arrest and was therefore aware of his own guilt. There were layers upon layers of corroborating testimony, medical testimony, meteorological testimony, but at its essence the commonwealth's case was this: Roy Smith killed Bessie Goldberg because no one else could have. And then he acted exactly like someone who had committed a murder but did not have the resources or the imagination to actually save himself afterward. He had simply avoided the inevitable as long as possible.

"You have the defendant here, Roy Smith, whose age is thirty-four years, thirty-five years," Kelley told the jury during his summation. "Five foot eleven, about 150 pounds, black hair, brown eyes, slim build, long sideburns and a moustache. And what else do we know about him? We have these pants—these clothes. There are holes in them; I ask you not to criticize the defendant at all for that; for poverty, no one can defend against. But there is nothing that a good bar of soap can't do. I'm not criticizing his sanitary habits, but I say this: In view of his drinking, is he a man of excessives? Now Mrs. Bessie Goldberg: A very hardworking, good housewife, was thrifty, a gentlewoman, without prejudices, who opened her home to this defendant . . . and that was repaid by the worst ingratitude conceivable: Death."

Kelley worked his way through Roy Smith's defense with the patient authority of a high school teacher grading term papers.

"Now, gentlemen, let us assume for the purposes of argument that what Roy Smith said at the police station is true; that he arrived at the Goldberg residence at quarter to twelve and left at quarter to four. The question is, then, who do you believe? Roy Smith at a quarter to twelve, or [witnesses] John Walsh, Antone Marcos and Robert Fitzgerald? They came here and were cross-examined and you heard their testimony . . . are they all in one grand conspiracy? Then let me ask you to consider in the light of that, the vile inferences that have been made about Mr. Goldberg. In addition to believing that Roy Smith did all that work in two hours, you have got to believe—and you have got to proclaim to the public—that Mr. Goldberg took time to find Mrs. Goldberg. Took time to throw her on the floor. Took time . . . to push her slip up. Took time to rip her pants and took time to have intercourse. Took time to put that stocking around her neck. Took time to hold it there, hold it, hold it until she was dead. And then after that, took time to move the sofa over. Took time to move the table away from the wall. Took time to put the various cleaning items, the brush, the cloths, on the bricbrac table. And then took time to leave. And they, the defense, make their vile inferences . . ."

Richard Kelley had served with the navy in the Pacific during World War II and was slated, along with his father, to be part of the force that was to attack mainland Japan. Richard Kelley was a man who was very clear—all law aside—on the concept of duty, on the concept of right and wrong. "Can any one of us go into the mind of a person that commits any crime of this nature and compare their standards of conduct with yours?" he asked. "Your standards, your backgrounds, your experiences are distant. Roy Smith had no money to go anyplace else. Was there anyone in the world that this man befriended enough to turn to? Much has been said through the whole trial that he wasn't nervous. Who is to say if he is nervous? Some people may be as cold as ice. Is this defendant in that category? Does he sit quietly and stoically in the box there without any show of emotion? If he is a man of little self-control, would he not stop at the first place for cigarettes after such an undertaking? It is a circumstantial case, gentlemen, and your duty is not an easy one. But I ask you this—"

No one on the jury knew what a difficult moment this must have been for Richard Kelley. He was from Boston. He was Irish. The terrible news had come into the courthouse just hours earlier, and he had delivered his entire summation knowing something that almost no one else in the room knew.

"I ask you this: In these times, do not be lacking in courage. Be true to yourselves, then you will be true to the defendant. You will be true to the people of the Commonwealth. You will be true to the laws we should all uphold. You sit in the capacity of fact-finders, and I urge each one of you that you leave here with the satisfaction that you will never look back and say, 'I did not perform the duty that was called upon me.'"

Richard Kelley sat down, and Judge Bolster turned to face Roy Smith. He told him that, since this was a capital case—one in which he could be put to death—he had the right to address the jury. "The privilege is yours," Judge Bolster said, "if you wish to avail yourself of it."

Roy Smith rose from his seat in the defendant's box. He had shaved his moustache and his sideburns and stood before the jury in his new suit under the high vaulted ceilings. Outside was a dull overcast day, waiting to rain, and the trees were already stripped of their leaves. Smith must have drawn a deep breath. He must have heard his voice shaking as he spoke his few words into the huge room. They would be the only words he would speak during the trial, and they would be perhaps the most important words of his life: "I would like to say to the court and jury," Smith said, "that I did not kill Mrs. Goldberg, or rob her, or rape her. She was alive when I left. Thank you."

The jury had been sequestered in a hotel for over two weeks, as was the custom at the time. They knew little of the recent events of the world and absolutely nothing of the events of that day. Judge Bolster turned in his seat to address the jury and spoke with all the solemnity of a judge and all the sorrow of an American: "Now I have a very sad duty, gentlemen; I don't know whether you have heard. Early this afternoon one or more assassins in Texas, apparently from high up in a building, fired shots at some of our officials. They hit the president, the vice president, and the governor of Texas, and the president, early this afternoon, died. I ask everyone in the room to rise."

The jury rose. Some were crying, others were simply in shock. Not only were half the jurors Irish, they were from Kennedy's original congressional district. It was as though they'd just learned that someone had killed their brother.

"I thought fast," Judge Bolster went on. "I am willing to take the responsibility. You have been here almost three weeks. I venture to think that if the president were here . . . he would do what I am doing. We are going ahead, but we are going ahead in a thoughtful sorrow about what has transpired. I have watched you gentlemen, and I think you are men of sufficient mental integrity not to let this influence you in any way in the decision of this case. This case is on its own evidence and on the arguments that have been ably presented to you, and so we are going forward. And will you please make every effort to be sure that your decision in this case is in no way tainted by the national disaster that has struck us. So you may retire, Mr. Foreman, and gentlemen, and we start at 8:30 in the morning."

With that, the trial of Roy Smith was over. Smith returned to his cell at Billerica House of Corrections and the jury returned to their hotel rooms and Judge Bolster and Beryl Cohen and Richard Kelley returned to their homes and their children and their wives. Each man waited out the long night with his particular worries or fears, but they all had one thing in common: The president of the United States was dead, and no one knew what would happen next.

FOURTEEN

THE PRESIDENT WAS hit in the neck and head by two bullets while riding in a motorcade through the city of Dallas, Texas. Seconds earlier the wife of the governor of Texas had turned to him and said, "You can't say Dallas doesn't love you." The shots were fired from a 6.5 mm Mannlicher-Carcano bolt-action rifle with a telescopic sight that Lee Harvey Oswald, the assassin, had bought for twenty-one dollars and change from a mail-order catalog. A spectator said that an "awful look" crossed the president's face when he was hit before he collapsed across the back of his open limo. Jackie crouched over him protectively, spattered in blood, as the motorcade raced for Parkland Memorial Hospital.

Doctors at Parkland gave the dying president blood and oxygen and even opened up his throat with a tracheotomy, but to no avail; around half an hour after the attack, Jackie kissed her husband on the lips for the last time and told the priest to pray over him. Father Oscar Huber commended the president's soul to God and then Kennedy was placed in a sealed bronze casket and loaded into a military ambulance. The ambulance pulled away with the drapes drawn shut and Jacqueline riding next to her dead husband. Ninety minutes had passed since they were waving happily to the crowds in downtown Dallas.

Kennedy was the youngest American president ever elected, the first American president born in the twentieth century, and the first American president to tackle aggressively what was effectively a system of apartheid in the southern states. He published a book the same year he graduated cum laude from Harvard University; he was nearly killed when a Japanese destroyer sliced his PT boat in half in the South Pacific during World War II; and he went on to publish a Pulitzer Prize–winning book before being elected president of the United States. He was so widely beloved that even in Moscow, women screamed in the streets when they heard the news of his death.

Vice President Lyndon Johnson, whom Kennedy had defeated in the Democratic primaries in 1960, had been riding two cars behind Kennedy when the shooting started. He was immediately driven to safety and then put on the presidential jet, where he was sworn in as president by a female judge who wept openly while administering the oath. Johnson's wife and Jackie Kennedy stood by his side as he raised his right hand and repeated the words that shifted the duties of the president onto him. The jet landed at Andrews Air Force Base at six o'clock that night, and Johnson stepped off the plane to face a throng of news reporters on the tarmac.

"I will do my best. That is all I can do," Johnson told reporters on the tarmac. "I ask for your help, and God's."

The casket bearing Kennedy's body was delivered from Bethesda Naval Hospital to the White House at four thirty the next morning. Hundreds of spectators who had stood vigil all night watched a blue-gray navy hearse pull up to the north portico in a heavy mist and stop in front of a detail of marines at present-arms. Jackie Kennedy stepped out of the hearse, her clothing still speckled with her husband's blood, and accompanied the casket with its marine escort into the White House. The casket was placed in the East Room atop a black-draped catafalque with a lit candle at each corner. Four servicemen representing each branch of the armed forces stood at attention with fixed bayonets. The casket was opened for Jackie to pay her last respects to her husband and then closed to receive the statesmen and dignitaries who had begun pouring into Washington from across the country and the world.

At ten thirty that morning a private ceremony was held around the casket for the Kennedy family and their closest friends, while elsewhere in the White House, workers tentatively began the task of packing up the Kennedy household. At eleven o'clock former president Eisenhower arrived by limousine and stepped bareheaded into a cold steady rain and walked into the north portico with his hat in his hand. He was followed by former president Harry Truman, House Speaker John McCormack, and the members of the Supreme Court, a ten-man honor guard jolting to attention every time another dignitary climbed the steps. At one o'clock that afternoon the casket was placed on an artillery caisson and drawn by six white horses, three of them riderless, to the Capitol Rotunda, where the body would lie in state throughout the night.

In Boston people were, if possible, in an even greater state of shock than in Washington. Services held Friday night at Saint Paul's Cathedral were attended by Governor Peabody and his wife, who was crying without restraint. Standing with the Peabodys, face frozen in shock, was the Reverend Harvey Cox, a good friend of the Kennedys who had just gotten out of jail in North Carolina. He had been arrested for leading a civil rights march. Telephone lines into and out of Boston were so overloaded that callers had to wait twenty minutes or more to get a dial tone. Scrubwomen at the State House on Beacon Hill sobbed as they went about their chores. Bartenders stepped outside their places of business to avoid crying in front of customers. Crowds of people gathered in front of newspaper offices to get the latest news.

The weather was cold, and by midday a slow steady rain had started to fall. The world had not ended but it had stumbled badly, and the people of Boston wandered around in the rain knowing they would have to go on living but not knowing exactly how.

AT EIGHT THIRTY Saturday morning—nineteen hours after the president was killed—the jury in the Roy Smith trial filed into the courtroom at Middlesex Superior Court and took their seats in the jury box. Every half hour people in Boston could hear the boom of a 105 mm howitzer on Boston Common that was being fired by the National Guard from dawn until dusk, in keeping with military tradition for the death of a president. Roy Smith was at his place in the defendant's dock, and Richard Kelley and a young assistant prosecutor named Ruth Abrams were at the prosecution table. Beryl Cohen was seated next to Roy Smith at his own table. Judge Bolster turned to the jury and told them that the case against Roy Smith was an entirely circumstantial one and that he would have to explain to them the nature of circumstantial evidence and how it can and can't be used in a court of law. The legal issues were so complex that Judge Bolster needed almost three hours to cover them.

"Circumstances must be such as to produce a moral certainty of guilt and to exclude any other reasonable hypothesis," he said, taking his language from a famous 1850 case called *Commonwealth v. Webster*. Webster was a Harvard professor who was accused of murdering someone who had loaned him money. He was convicted—and eventually hanged in public—on evidence that was purely circumstantial. "The circumstances taken together should be of a conclusive nature and tendency," the judge went on, "leading on the whole to a satisfactory conclusion and producing . . . a reasonable and moral certainty that the accused, and no one else, committed the crime."

Circumstantial evidence is everything except eyewitness testimony, photographs, and other evidence from the crime itself, which is called direct evidence. Direct evidence is extremely powerful as long as it is supported by circumstantial evidence; unsupported, it is only as reliable as the witness who supplies it. Eyewitnesses are famously inaccurate; they have lied on the stand, misremembered things, imagined things, and reinvented reality whole cloth. Studies have shown, for example, that people of one race have a much harder time correctly identifying people of another race. Studies have also shown that casually mentioning a nonexistent object during a conversation—during police interviews of witnesses, for example—increases the likelihood that a person later "remembers" seeing it by 15 percent. Stress affects memory as well, and violence is extremely stressful. Muskets have been found on Civil War battlefields with dozens of cartridges in their barrels, rammed home by soldiers who were too terrified to remember to fire each time they reloaded. Witnesses to violent crimes can be similarly unaware of their actions.

Circumstantial evidence, on the other hand, uses known facts to draw inferences about unknown facts. No single fact is enough to prove guilt—the defendant was observed near the scene of the crime, for example—but taken together, they prove the defendant is guilty. When judges instruct a jury on circumstantial evidence, they sometimes use the example of a law clerk arriving at work in the morning to find the judge's coat hanging in the closet, a cup of hot coffee on his desk, and the morning paper open next to it. The clerk does not need to actually see the judge with his own eyes to conclude that he is almost certainly in the building. The weakness of circumstantial evidence is that, ultimately, it is an extremely complex form of guesswork that involves dozens of interrelated facts, but that is also its strength: Dozens of interrelated facts are thought almost never to arrange themselves in such a way to make an innocent man look guilty.

To refute a circumstantial case, all the defense ordinarily has to do is break *one* link in a chain of inferences created by the prosecution. The defense attacks all up and down the line, of course, hoping for breakthroughs everywhere, but all they need is one solid break. Halfway through his summation, Beryl Cohen had pointed out a detail that the jury surely missed when they heard it: A practical nurse working on Scott Road testified that one of the children who saw Israel Goldberg arrive home had stepped off the school bus on one corner of Pleasant Street, when in fact she had gotten off on a different corner. "It's not a big victory," Cohen admitted to the jury. "Lawyers don't win cases on the little things. But you get enough little things, you may get a reasonable doubt. You get a reasonable doubt in a circumstantial case, watch for the strict proof, watch for the presumption of innocence."

Cohen's summation had shied away from a grand theory of innocence for Smith and instead went for a blizzard of particulars. Smith was not avoiding arrest in Cambridge, Cohen claimed; he was simply looking for his girlfriend, Carol Bell. The next morning

Smith accompanied Dorothy Hunt as she took her daughter to the optometrist, which required walking directly past the Cambridge police station in Central Square. Sidewalk vendors were already selling newspapers that identified Roy Smith as a fugitive who was wanted for the murder of Bessie Goldberg. Was this the behavior of a guilty man, of a man who was evading arrest? Cohen went on to point out that no one who encountered Smith that afternoon thought he looked nervous except Louis Pizzuto, who had misidentified the clothing Smith was wearing and seemed to be a racist anyway.

"And we had a lady named Geneva Harden, the landlady at 175 Northampton Street," Cohen had told the jury. "She came on and testified that the defendant didn't need any particular money in terms of rent. Wasn't behind in his rent. And then of course there was a stakeout. Do you mark a Boston police officer's car and put it in front of 175 Northampton Street? Put the lights on in the apartment and sit there and watch television and wait? Anyone walking down the street is going to see the scene and say, 'Not tonight. Think I'll sleep out.' "

According to Cohen the police had actually made themselves comfortable in Smith's apartment while they waited for him; even an innocent person might hesitate to go into the apartment under those circumstances. Cohen went on to question how long Goldberg was really inside the house as well as his response to the crime, which was to call the police rather than an ambulance. "What can I say?" Cohen asked. "Can I summon in my mind a man married a number of years who comes home, finds his wife lying on the ground and does not put his hand to her head? Didn't go near her? Didn't touch a thing—didn't even try to loosen the scarf?"

The crucial testimony, though, was from the children. Because of them it was supposedly known that Goldberg had spent only a couple of minutes in his house and that no one else had gone in or out. But Cohen questioned whether children playing kickball on the street could monitor even the front door of a house, much less a back door facing a yard enclosed by bushes. Cohen went on to accuse Kelley of feeding the children whatever testimony he needed while preparing them for the trial. "The district attorney became a schoolteacher!" Cohen proclaimed. "He had them in the other courtroom one at a time, he went over their testimony. I just stumbled on it: I asked Susan Faunce, 'Have you ever seen that exhibit before?' And she said, 'Yes, last Wednesday.' Gentlemen of the jury, she saw that exhibit before I did! And I have the obligation to try a capital case!"

Cohen dismissed the testimony of Smith's friends as far too compromised by alcoholism and legal troubles to be trusted. He dismissed the fact that the state police chemist had found a small semen stain on Smith's pants because the jury was not allowed to inspect the pants for themselves. He dismissed Smith's entire interrogation in the Belmont police station—upon which the commonwealth based the bulk of their case—because it was coercive and unfair. He was referring to the fact that John Droney, the Middlesex County DA, had told the Belmont police chief to go have dinner in Cambridge while Smith was being interrogated.

"The district attorney made the Belmont Police Department look like a little boy with a lollipop!" Cohen told the jury. "He was told to get out of the station—'We'll use your room, go out to dinner.' And who came in but the big-city boys. I do not suggest they put their hands on the defendant—no evidence of that. But you have to realize that when these detectives, the big boys from the city, when they interrogate a prisoner they know the rules of evidence.

They know about the admissibility of evidence, and when the poor guy who didn't do it gets caught up with the big-city boys, watch out. No confession from the defendant. He withstood it. I don't say they won't put their hands on him, there are no false issues here. But there is such a thing called coercion. Being at that desk for ten or twelve hours . . . that could be called coercion, under the right circumstances."

Cohen finished in a blaze of indignation: "Smith is here on the basis of murder, rape, and robbery. Are you going to take his life? You have it within your hands tomorrow afternoon. Are you going to take his life on the basis of the people at the country club? Are you going to take his life on the basis of the children who 'attended school' with the district attorney? Are you going to take his life on the basis of evidence that was evolved in a police station? Have courage! I know you will!"

This was a jury's dilemma at its most terrible: to decide between two plausible but utterly contradictory propositions. Either Roy Smith killed Bessie Goldberg but was too apathetic to conceal it—failing even to get rid of her address in his pocket—or he didn't kill Bessie Goldberg and was the victim of bad luck and the distortions of the Middlesex DA's office. Furthermore, in some criminal cases it is possible to be found guilty of some crimes and not others, but this case was all or nothing. Either Smith killed, raped, and robbed Bessie Goldberg or did none of those things; logically Smith could not be innocent of one of those crimes and not of the others. The man who killed Bessie Goldberg also raped her; if the rape was not plausible, then neither was the murder. And neither crime would have happened without the robbery, which was described by Richard Kelley as the motivation for the murder in the first place.

Even Beryl Cohen would have to admit that Smith made an

excellent suspect in the murder of Bessie Goldberg, but that wasn't the question before the jury. The question was whether Roy Smith *killed* Bessie Goldberg, not whether he *could* have killed her. In a civil case—in which a man's life or liberty is not at stake—the jury uses something called a "preponderance of evidence" to decide whether something is true. The jury only has to decide if something is more likely than *not* likely to be true; the chances have to be at least slightly better than fifty-fifty. By that standard a jury could easily find Roy Smith guilty of killing Bessie Goldberg.

In a criminal trial, however, a jury cannot send someone to prison—or, in Smith's case, to the electric chair—unless he is guilty "beyond a reasonable doubt." It is a phrase that almost everyone thinks they understand but no one can explain. The classic definition was penned Chief Justice Lemuel Shaw, who incorporated it into his instructions on circumstantial evidence in the 1850 *Webster* case. "What is reasonable doubt?" Shaw asked. "It is not a mere possible doubt; because everything relating to human affairs, and depending on moral evidence, is open to some possible or imaginary doubt. It is not sufficient to establish a probability, though a strong one, that the fact charged is more likely to be true than the contrary. The evidence must establish the truth of the fact to a reasonable and moral certainty."

Trying to define "reasonable doubt" is like trying to define a color; you end up having to explain the very words you use in your definition. If a jury doesn't intuitively understand the phrase "reasonable doubt," they're not going to be helped much by the term "moral certainty." Over the years, courts have struggled to clarify, in some senses, the obvious: "It is not a fanciful doubt, it is not an imagined doubt, and it is not a doubt a juror might conjure up to avoid performing an unpleasant duty," Black's Law Dictionary offered. Nor is it "free-floating existential doubt," a legal scholar added. One court finally acknowledged that there may be no better definition of the phrase "than the phrase itself."

The central problem with the idea of reasonable doubt—with the entire premise of man-made justice—is that it tries to determine an objective truth with subjective tools. It will never be known in any absolute sense whether Roy Smith killed Bessie Goldberg; that is simply a given, the starting point of any determination of Smith's guilt. Lacking the ability to "see men as God does," as one legal scholar put it, the courts must settle for some lesser version of the truth. That lesser version is known as "legal" guilt. It is possible to be actually innocent—to have truly not killed Bessie Goldberg— and to still be found legally guilty of her murder. Legal guilt simply means that twelve unbiased people heard the evidence against you and decided that you killed Bessie Goldberg beyond any reasonable doubt. Maybe you did *not* kill her but—strictly speaking—that is not a concern of the court. The concern of the court is that you receive justice, and justice is defined as having received a fair trial. Fair trials, in turn, have been described in the Constitution; everything else is in the hands of the jury.

The disadvantage of this system is that innocent people can be found guilty and put to death. Between 1973 and 2000, more than one hundred people have been released from death row—over 3 percent of the current death-row population—because they were later proved to be innocent. As one defense attorney noted, the Federal Aviation Administration would never tolerate an airline that lost one plane out of a hundred; why should the justice system? DNA evidence, which was not available until 1989, was responsible for thirteen of the exonerations. With an error rate as low as one in a trillion, DNA evidence is virtually all-powerful in court and can win convictions with almost no supporting evidence. If it can send people to the electric chair, though, it can also save them from it, and that is a power that state prosecutors are loath give up. One case that wound up before the Missouri Supreme Court involved a man who was due to be executed despite the chance that a court-ordered DNA test would prove he was innocent. The assistant district attorney in the case argued that the new evidence should not be considered by the court. The presiding judge, Michael Wolff, was incredulous.

"To make sure we're clear on this," Judge Wolff asked, "if we find that DNA evidence absolutely excludes somebody as the murderer, then we must execute them anyway?"

The answer, according to the assistant DA, was yes. A jury had determined that the man was legally guilty, and if the state began to question jury decisions, the whole system would fall apart. You don't endanger the ship to save one drowning sailor, in other words. Ultimately the gap between legal guilt and actual guilt is the gap between human perception and objective truth, and that is a gap that has ruined lives—and tormented philosophers—for millennia. In a famous parable the Greek philosopher Plato described a cave where bound prisoners are held in complete darkness except for a campfire behind them that projects shadows on the wall. The shadows were made by passing objects in front of the fire. Everything these men knew about reality was based on the shadows; the objects themselves remained unknowable and maybe even unimaginable. *That* is a modern jury. They are allowed to see evidence from the crime, but they can never turn their heads to see the crime itself. They must come to a conclusion based only on the evidence—the shadows—that they are allowed to see.

"This is a strange picture," the Socratic student Glaucon com-mented after hearing about the cave for the first time. "And strange prisoners."

At 11:25 a.m. on November 23, 1963, twelve such strange prisoners retired to a jury room in the Middlesex Superior Courthouse to decide whether Roy Smith had, in fact, killed Bessie Goldberg.

FIFTEEN

TWENTY MILES TO the north in the failing mill town of Lawrence, Massachusetts, the phone was ringing in the apartment of a twenty-three-year-old woman named Joann Graff. Graff lived alone in a one-room apartment and worked in an industrial design shop; on Sundays she taught classes at a local church. Graff answered the phone and spoke for a few moments to a friend named Mrs. Johnson, who invited her to dinner that night with some other families from their congregation. Graff favored plain dresses and wire-rim glasses, and a last-minute invitation to a Saturday-night church dinner was about as spontaneous as she ever got. She said yes and hung up the phone.

One hour later—at 12:30 in the afternoon—Graff's landlord knocked on the door. Graff opened up and gave him the fifteen dollars' rent and then closed the door behind her. In the time that the door was open, though, the landlord noticed that the breakfast dishes were done and that a religious book lay open on the kitchen table. At some point in the next three hours but probably toward the end of that period, a second person knocked on Joann Graff's door. She must have let the person in, because Graff's neighbors heard nothing through the thin rooming-house walls. Whoever the intruder was, he knew what he was doing. He forced Graff diagonally across her own bed without the neighbors hearing, and he twisted two stockings and a black leotard around her neck without the neighbors hearing, and finally he stripped her and raped her and killed her without her neighbors hearing anything at all. Then he ransacked the apartment—though he left money for the gas bill sitting untouched on the kitchen table—and closed the apartment door behind him when he left.

The police were able to pinpoint the time of the murder to within minutes. A Northeastern University student named Ken Rowe, who lived one floor above Graff, told police that at 3:25 that afternoon, a man in a brown jacket and green pants had knocked on his door and asked where Graff lived. Rowe said the man looked like he was in his late twenties and wore his hair carefully combed back with grease. Rowe directed the man downstairs and shut the door. At that point Graff was presumably still alive.

Five minutes later Mrs. Johnson picked up the phone and started dialing Joann Graff's number. It was exactly 3:30 in the afternoon. In Cambridge the jurors in the Roy Smith case were just closing in on an agreement about his guilt. In Boston a National Guard gunner was locking a 105 mm round into the breach of a howitzer and waiting for permission to fire. By the time the thud of the concussion had died out, Joann Graff's phone had stopped ringing, and another Boston woman was dead.

AT 4:50 THAT same afternoon, the members of the Smith jury, led by foreman Jim Bird, filed into Judge Bolster's courtroom and took their seats. Both alternate jurors had been dismissed from the case because they were no longer needed. Roy Smith sat unshackled in his locked defendant's box with Beryl Cohen near him at the defense table and his mother, Mollie Smith, and his twenty-two-year-old sister, Betty, behind him in the front row. (Cohen had bought their plane tickets and found them a place to stay with a friend of his for the duration of the trial.) Cohen had undoubtedly told Smith that if the jury returned a guilty verdict he would use President Kennedy's assassination as the basis of an appeal. Attorneys believe they can read a jury's verdict on their faces, and both Cohen and Kelley must have scrutinized the jurors as they walked in. Jurors who keep their eyes lowered and avoid looking at the defendant come bearing bad news, lawyers believe; it is no different in the courtroom than in life.

The clerk of the court asked the jury and the defendant to rise, and Beryl Cohen and Roy Smith and the twelve men of the jury got to their feet. Rain tapped against the tall windows. The court officer asked the jury whether they had reached a verdict, and the foreman said that they had.

What say you, Mr. Foreman? the court officer demanded. Do you find the defendant guilty or not guilty?

Guilty, foreman Bird responded.

Of what crimes? the clerk demanded.

Of murder in the first degree, Bird responded.

Bird told the court that the jury had also found the defendant, Roy Smith, guilty of the charge of larceny but innocent of the charge of rape. There is nothing in the law that insists a verdict must be logical, so Richard Kelley could not challenge the jury on the rape acquittal. Smith could have gone to the electric chair if they had found otherwise, so it may have been a compromise verdict that reflected some doubt about his guilt. When a jury departs from the evidence and delivers a verdict that reflects some broader sense of justice, it is called "jury nullification." Juries have used nullification to spare white men who were obviously guilty of lynching blacks, as well as to spare battered women who were obviously guilty of killing their husbands. Jury nullification, although treated warily by the courts, has traditionally been one way in which the "conscience of the community" can counteract the effect of an unpopular law.

Jury verdicts are not open to questioning by the court, so there was no way to find out why Smith was exonerated of the rape or how the jury resolved in their minds the logical problems that gave rise to. Foreman Bird did, however, make a point of recommending that Smith not be sentenced to death. After the verdict was read, Smith remained standing but was described by newspaper reporters in the courtroom as "visibly shaken." Leah Goldberg thought he looked utterly impassive, as though he expected this and didn't much care. The court quickly moved to sentence, and then Smith was handcuffed by the bailiff and led past his mother and sister, both of whom were sobbing, and past the lawyers and court clerks and the rest of the spectators.

At 5:30 on the afternoon of November 23, 1963, Smith walked out of the building under a cold rain to begin serving a term of life imprisonment without the possibility of parole.

SIXTEEN

TWELVE WOMEN WERE strangled and beaten to death in their homes over the course of a year and a half in the Boston area, and only one of the murders—Bessie Goldberg—was considered solved. Logically the remaining murders were committed either by one skilled murderer or many lucky ones. During the early sixties three out of four Boston homicides resulted in an arrest, and roughly 60 percent of those arrests resulted in a conviction. After a year and a half and the biggest manhunt in Massachusetts history, the eleven remaining Boston stranglings had an arrest rate of zero and a conviction rate of zero. The numbers were way, way off the bell curve, particularly for a city that had been on high alert for the past year and a half. Murderers are often impulsive, psychologically unstable people who, among other things, are not particularly good at thinking ahead. The ones who are, like Ted Bundy, quickly achieve legendary status for their ability to kill virtually anywhere at any time. The rest—like Roy Smith—are usually arrested within days.

During the eighteen months of "Boston stranglings," three other women were also strangled who did not quite fit the pattern. One, a sixteen-year-old black girl named Donna Saunders, was found manually strangled in a back alley in Boston. Another was a sixty-year-old "heavy drinker" named Margaret Davis who was found manually strangled in a cheap hotel room. The third was a thirty-seven-year-old black woman named Modeste Freeman who was found nude in someone's backyard, strangled to death with a sweater and beaten almost beyond recognition. None of these murders were considered classic "Boston Stranglings" because the victims were found outside their homes. By comparison, however, two of those three murders were solved within days: Saunders was killed by a high school boy who was furious because she wouldn't kiss him, and Davis was killed by a man she met in a bar and went with to the hotel.

A success rate of two out of three is typical for a homicide unit in an American city; one out of twelve is not. Statistics alone would argue that there was a single skilled killer out there, but the great diversity of victims—old, young, black, white—would argue against it. Much of what was known about the psychology of sexual predators pointed to at least two men, one who killed older women and one who killed younger ones. Part of the problem in establishing a pattern was that the murders spanned a patchwork of town, city, and county jurisdictions, and the various authorities involved were unable—and reluctant—to share information. Without a careful analysis of all the crime scenes, investigators could never hope to create a psychological profile of the killer or, conversely, demonstrate that it was the work of several men.

The inefficiency of the investigators was rewarded one final time January 4, when a young white woman named Mary Sullivan was

found strangled in her Beacon Hill apartment. Sullivan had graduated from high school on Cape Cod a year earlier and had moved to
Boston to work as a secretary in a financial firm. Her two teenage
roommates arrived home around six o'clock on a snowy evening to
find their dead friend propped up in bed with a leotard and two
scarves tied around her neck and a broom handle shoved into her
vagina. A greeting card that had been placed by her left foot read
"Happy New Year!" The scarves she had been strangled with were
brightly colored and done up in huge bows, as if she were someone's
birthday present, and her legs were spread apart to shock her dis-
coverer as much as possible. Mary Sullivan was nineteen years old.

The public outrage had still not died down two weeks later when
Ed Brooke, the attorney general of Massachusetts, announced that
his office was taking over the investigation of the Boston Strangling
cases. Brooke had managed, as a Republican in a staunchly
Democratic state, to become the highest elected black official—and
the only black attorney general—in the country. No longer would
the murders fall under nine separate jurisdictions within the state,
Brooke announced; they would now be handled by a new office
called the Special Division of Crime Research and Detection. To the
people of Boston the special division quickly became known as the
Strangler Bureau.

The Strangler Bureau was headed by an independently wealthy
Bostonian named John Bottomly, who had graduated from
Deerfield Academy and Harvard and gone on to head the Eminent
Domain Division of the Attorney General's Office. Bottomly had
absolutely no experience in criminal investigations but was a fero-
ciously methodical man who was not intimidated by the 37,500
pages of documentation that had been generated by the ongoing
investigation. It was a stack of paper ten feet high that, somewhere,

held the secret of who was killing and raping women in Boston; Bottomly just had to be clever enough to see it.

Taking direction from Bottomly was Michael Cullinane, acting captain of state police detectives, Lt. John Donovan, head of Boston Homicide, Lt. Andrew Tuney of the Essex County DA's office, and Detectives Phil DiNatale and James Mellon of the Boston police. They were joined later in the spring of 1964 by a low-ranking metropolitan police officer named Steve Delaney who had taken an amateur interest in the strangling cases. Delaney had gotten hold of a spreadsheet of all the murders and spent his spare time playing detective with the cases, trying to see patterns. One day Cullinane asked Delaney whether he thought the stranglings were the work of one man or several, and Delaney answered without hesitation that they were the work of one man. Cullinane asked why. Well, Delaney said, the murders had happened in half a dozen different police jurisdictions, all of which had an excellent record for solving murders, and none of them had been solved. That, to Delaney, suggested the work of one very sick and skillful murderer. Attorney General Brooke got wind of this demonstration of logic and asked Cullinane why he had to hear it from a beat cop instead of a homicide detective. Cullinane's response was to give Delaney a spot on the Strangler Bureau.

The murder files were kept in a vault at the Eminent Domain Office in the State House, just off Boston Common. Photographs of the murder scenes and lists of evidence were pinned to a board that was kept facing away from the vault entrance so that people who stopped in would not have to see them. Investigators like Delaney could walk around to the other side and see, at a glance, the entire sweep of the city's tragedy. Delaney was given the job of sorting through the crime scene reports to determine if there was a pattern to the killings. It was an overwhelming task: The Eminent Domain Office was filled with scores of cardboard boxes, and each box was packed with files that no one had gone through yet. Within weeks, though, Delaney came to the conclusion that there was an unmistakable pattern among the killings—one that pointed to a single killer. His opinion was echoed by a little-known FBI report that came out several years later and was based on a much-less-hurried analysis. "All of the murders and assaults happened at multiple dwelling apartments with brick fronts, of transient character where many people were constantly coming and going," the report stated. "There were always two or three exits to these apartment houses. Ninety percent of these apartment houses were sorely in need of repairs in one way or another. The victim was positioned so that, upon entering the room from any door, the body would be in full view. The sexual organs were noticed and the legs spread apart."

Without exception the women had also died in their own homes after apparently letting their killer in voluntarily and putting up little, if any, struggle. It was as if the killer or killers were able to gain entry under some pretext and then attack the women from behind, when they could offer no defense. The attacks were quiet and deadly and probably over in minutes. Some women were sexually assaulted with objects and others were raped and still others bore injuries to their breasts, but none was grossly mutilated. The point of these crimes was sexual humiliation, and murder was an unavoidable result of that process. This was not a disorganized killer who was obeying voices in his head; this was a completely functional killer who walked out onto the street afterward and had no problem blending in with the people around him. This was a man who could be married, have a job, raise children—a man who, ultimately, was outwardly indistinguishable from the detectives who were trying to catch him.

One of the more distracting theories was that one of the killers might be a homosexual, which led detectives to throw a blanket of scrutiny over clubs that catered to that clientele. According to Delaney, police officers infiltrated known homosexual bars, hoping to hear something about the murders, and wrote down the license plate numbers of cars parked in the area. One particularly obsessed investigator gathered so much data on homosexual nightlife that he single-handedly began to slow down the investigation. He was finally issued a cease-and-desist order. Another distracting theory was that the murders couldn't possibly be the work of one man. A single uncatchable man was far more embarrassing to the police than a crime wave, and as a result there was reluctance on the part of police investigators—particularly Lt. John Donovan—to see links between the crimes.

Donovan, however, had his own theories on the apparent pattern in the killings. The victims were always women, he said, not because there was a lone, woman-obsessed killer out there, but simply because women are more likely to be the target of sexual attacks. The women were killed in their homes because that is where they were most likely to be found alone. There were no screams because the women were being strangled, and they were strangled with stockings, leotards, and scarves because those things could easily be found on the woman who was being attacked.

Police did have one thing going for them, and that was a possible description of at least one if the killers. Joann Graff's upstairs neighbor told police that the man who knocked on his door shortly before the murder was in his late twenties, of medium build, and wearing green pants and a dark jacket. That almost exactly described the man who had knocked on Marcella Lulka's door shortly before the Sophie Clark murder a year earlier; the only difference was that Lulka had remembered the man's hair as "honey-colored" rather than dark. Neither of those people had actually been attacked, but their descriptions also matched that of the suspect in a sexual attack in Boston that had all the signs of a failed Boston Strangling. Around noon on February 18, 1963, a German-born waitress named Erika Wilsing got up to answer a knock on her apartment door and was confronted by a dark-haired man in his midthirties who said he was there to check her apartment for leaks. The man was wearing a waist-length jacket and green work pants and was of medium height and a muscular build. Wilsing let the man in and turned her back for a moment; the next thing she knew, he had her down on the floor with an arm across her throat. Wilsing was a big, strong woman, and she managed to lock her jaws on one of his fingers. The attacker loosened his grip long enough for her to scream, which got the attention of some workmen on a neighboring roof. Moments later her attacker was gone.

A police illustrator drew a sketch of the killer based on those descriptions, but it didn't even lead to a suspect, much less to an arrest. It was a measure of the bureau's desperation (or incompetence, depending on whom you asked) that they reached way out beyond the bounds of ordinary police work. A psychic named Paul Gordon had previously told police that a very disturbed young man named Arnold Wallace, who was suspected in his own mother's death, was also the Boston Strangler. Gordon was given an injection of sodium amytal, which induces a state similar to hypnosis, and was questioned extensively by several members of the Strangler Bureau. Gordon's testimony about the crime scenes was at times wildly off and at times strangely accurate. Among other things, he described a photograph of a ballerina hanging in Ida Irga's apartment that had never been mentioned in the press. One possibility that the investigators considered was that Gordon himself was the murderer but didn't consciously realize it, and was only able to talk about it under a chemically induced hypnosis. The other possibility was that he was in fact psychic—whatever that meant—and that Arnold Wallace was indeed the killer, but investigators were never able to link him to the murders in any convincing way.

Within weeks of Brooke's announcement, the newly formed Strangler Bureau invited another, more famous psychic to Boston. Peter Hurkos was a Dutch Jew who said that he had become psychic very abruptly after injuring his head in a fall from a ladder. The accident had happened in the midst of World War II, and Hurkos claimed that his new "radar brain" helped him evade the Nazis after they overran Holland. "I see pictures, like on TV," Hurkos explained. "I cannot help them, they come and go in my brain. They show me what I'm looking for." After the war was over Hurkos applied his strange powers to solving murders and missing-persons cases and eventually wound up in Los Angeles to work on a movie about psychics. Hurkos was an enthusiastic self-promoter who had already put one innocent man in custody for a multiple murder committed by someone else. Three weeks after Mary Sullivan's murder, he flew into Providence, Rhode Island, and was driven by John Bottomly to a hotel outside Boston, where he checked in under a false name.

Like Gordon, Hurkos was inexplicably correct on several details of the crimes known only to the police. The focus of his suspicions was a lonely door-to-door shoe salesman named Daniel Moran who had already caught the attention of the police for writing odd, threatening letters to women. Moran was unquestionably disturbed; he tried to join a monastery but was refused, he supposedly showered with his shoes on, and he had once told his personal physician he was worried that he was out killing women during periodic blackouts. He confessed to nothing when police detained him, though, and in due time his alibis proved to be largely unassailable.

It was thought that whoever was doing the killing probably had some prior history of misbehavior, but that opened up an enormous investigatory task. There were thousands of men in the Boston area who had crossed some line with the female sex, and they all had to be tracked down and evaluated as suspects. A disturbed young man from Belmont was picked up after nurses at a hospital caught him trying to look into the ladies' room. He quickly confessed to killing Beverly Samans in May 1963, but he got his facts sufficiently mixed up that the police had to release him. A married woman called in her suspicions about a man who lived in her apartment building, but it turned out she'd been having an affair with him and was enraged when he called it off. An extremely violent psychotic who had attacked two elderly women in the towns of Salem and Peabody was questioned in the strangling death of an elderly woman named Evelyn Corbin, but the only physical evidence linking him to the crime was a half-eaten doughnut on Corbin's fire escape. The man had eaten doughnuts for breakfast that day, but that wasn't enough evidence to bring charges. A paranoid schizophrenic who washed dishes in a restaurant a block from Mary Sullivan's apartment was also questioned and released, and a black man who knew Sophie Clark—and had a secret life as a homosexual—was given a lie detector test and released despite the fact that he had flunked it badly. Detectives had extremely good reason to suspect some of these men, but they could not arrest them without a confession or strong physical evidence. A doughnut on a fire escape or a failed lie detector test was not, in and of itself, proof that someone had committed a crime.

SEVENTEEN

WHILE BOSTON WAS trying to track down a serial killer, America was slowly emerging from its fog of grief. The murder of the president, as it turned out, was not just a low point in an otherwise upward-trending time for the country; it was the lip of a long slide into turmoil. Early in 1964 Congress passed the Tonkin Gulf Resolution, which authorized President Johnson to use "all necessary measures" to protect U.S. forces abroad. Within months Johnson had ordered air strikes against North Vietnamese forces in response to attacks against the American base in Pleiku. At home racial issues were coming closer to dividing the country than anytime since the Civil War. Dr. Martin Luther King's nonviolent tactics started to gain adherence among black activists, but an ex-convict named Malcolm X dismissed them out of hand. "If you think I'll bleed nonviolently, you'll be sticking me for the rest of my life," Malcolm X said. "But if I tell you I'll fight back, there'll be less blood. I'm for reciprocal bleeding."

Malcolm X went on to promise that 1964 would be the "hottest summer in history," and it came close. In June, King was jailed in St. Augustine, Florida, for trying to eat at a segregated lunch counter. A few weeks later three civil rights workers in Mississippi were killed by a deputy sheriff and a part-time Baptist minister and buried in an earth levee near Philadelphia, Mississippi. Then, in July, riots ignited in Harlem after a New York City police officer shot and killed a fifteen-year-old black boy who was carrying a knife. An angry mob surrounded the precinct house after word of the killing got out, and the police chief had to call for reinforcements to keep from getting overrun. Gunfire was so heavy up Lenox Avenue that night that reporters said it sounded as if police were shooting automatic weapons. The violence sputtered on for days.

Northern reporters went down to the Mississippi Delta to cover the civil rights movement as if they were going to Vietnam to cover the war, not knowing whether they'd make it back. One photographer who had gotten chased by a carload of white thugs found it necessary to buy at 12-gauge shotgun and continue his reporting with the gun across his lap. Meanwhile enlightened ideas about race seemed to be making some headway in the upper echelons of government. Congress passed the Civil Rights Act, which gave the federal government broad powers to combat racism at the state level. In November 1964, Lyndon Johnson used that issue to win the presidential election against Barry Goldwater, who, despite the fact that he was half Jewish, was utterly opposed to the antidiscrimination measures in Congress.

In early 1965, an article in *Look* magazine quoted Malcolm X as saying that the debate between violence and nonviolence was, in reality, a debate between self-defense and masochism. In late February, Malcolm X was gunned down in a Harlem ballroom by three young black men who were then nearly beaten to death by the crowd. Two weeks later, riot police in Selma, Alabama, decimated a peaceful protest march with tear gas and nightsticks under orders from Governor George Wallace, who vehemently opposed black voter registration and new federal antisegregation measures. The attack backfired, not only bringing Dr. King to Selma, but promoting a speech by President Johnson before Congress that was interrupted thirty-six times by applause. Johnson told Congress that the country had waited more than a hundred years for true freedom and that the time for waiting was gone. "There is no Negro problem, there is no Southern problem, there is no Northern problem," he declared. "There is only an American problem. There's really no part of America where the promise of equality has been fully kept."

The date was March 15, 1965. Television cameras showed some congressmen moved nearly to tears and others slumped in their seats like recalcitrant schoolboys. Johnson blew kisses to his wife as he finished his speech and strode out of the chamber. A new era in America had begun.

IT WAS SOMETIME in early March—between the Selma riots and Johnson's historic speech—that the phone rang in our house, and when my mother answered it, she was surprised to hear Russ Blomerth on the line. Russ hadn't called in two years—not since the studio had been finished—but he had odd and urgent news. Mrs. Junger, he told her, I don't know how to tell you this. But I've just found out that Al DeSalvo is the Boston Strangler.

There was only one telephone in our house, a white rotary desk phone that sat on a shelf by the entrance to the kitchen, and next to the shelf there was a small stool. My mother felt her knees go out from under her, and the next thing she knew, she was sitting on the stool. She had never told Russ about the incident with Al in the basement—she'd never even told my father—but now it all came back to her.

He was just caught on a rape case, Blomerth went on. And then he confessed to being the Boston Strangler.

Blomerth presumably wanted my mother to hear the news from him before she read it in the newspaper. DeSalvo had begun making lengthy confessions to the police, and Blomerth had already been contacted by investigators to provide corroborating evidence. DeSalvo, as it turned out, had been alone or off the clock for every single strangling in the Boston area. The authorities were particularly interested in December 5 and December 30, 1962, which were the days Sophie Clark and Patricia Bissette had been killed. Blomerth said his records showed that on those days, Al had come to our house by himself to check on the diesel heaters. "The exact hours that he did this I have no way of knowing," Blomerth testified in writing. "But I must tell you that Albert was a truly remarkable man. He had unbelievable strength, energy and endurance. He was completely lovable to every individual while working for me. Never was there any deviation from the highest proper sense of things."

So Al had left our house and gone on to kill a young woman. Or he had killed a young woman and then showed up to work twenty minutes later; either possibility was too horrifying to contemplate. Al had spent many, many days working in the studio while my mother was home alone; all he'd had to do was ask to use the bathroom or the telephone, and he was inside the house with her. It would be stupid to kill someone you were working for—you'd be an immediate suspect, like Roy Smith—but couldn't you do it on a day when no one knew you were there? Al came to our house to check the heaters unannounced and on no particular schedule. What would have prevented him from attacking my mother and then slipping away afterward?

My mother hung up the phone and shuffled through her memories of DeSalvo. What about the afternoon when Bessie Goldberg was killed; could Al have driven over to Scott Road—which he passed every day on his commute from his home in Malden—and killed her and then gone back to work? My mother had come home that day to a phone call from my baby-sitter telling her to lock the doors because the Boston Strangler had just killed someone nearby. She had hung up the phone and gone in back to repeat the bad news to Al, who was painting trim on a stepladder. What could have possibly been going through Al's mind during that conversation? If he was indeed the Strangler but hadn't killed Bessie Goldberg, it must have been a terrific shock to hear about a similar crime so close by. And if he *had* killed Bessie Goldberg, there my mother stood at the foot of the ladder telling him about it. How would my mother—alone in the house with dusk falling and a dead woman down the road—have appeared to the man who had just committed the murder?

Four months earlier Al had stood at the bottom of the cellar stairs and called up to my mother with an odd look in his eyes. For a moment, at least, our basement was a place where the very worst things imaginable could happen without anyone around to prevent them. Was there some equivalent place in Al's mind where he went in those moments—some dark cellar hole filled with dead women and a staircase leading back up into the rest of his life? If so, why had he not gone down there, figuratively speaking, while my mother stood in the studio talking about the latest murder? What had protected her from the fate that those other women had suffered?

There was no way to know; my mother just remembered Al

saying how terrible it was about the Goldberg murder and then going back to painting trim. By seven o'clock that night, my father had returned from work and was hearing from my mother what had happened on Scott Road that day. Dr. Edwin Hill of the Harvard University Department of Legal Medicine was snapping on his latex gloves at the Short and Williamson Funeral Home and commencing the autopsy on Bessie Goldberg's body. Al was already at home with his wife and children. Roy Smith was drinking cheap whiskey in a Central Square apartment and either worrying about the fact that he'd just committed murder or—if he hadn't—worrying about how he was going to convince the police of that.

And Leah and Israel Goldberg, still deeply in shock, were answering endless questions at 14 Scott Road. They had not yet started out across a continent of grief that a lifetime of walking could not cover.

THE
CONFESSIONS

EIGHTEEN

Albert DeSalvo, Bridgewater Correctional Institution: "That day of the first one, it was in summer of 1962 and I think it was raining or going to rain because I remember I had a raincoat with me. I told my wife I was going fishing and I took my rod and a fishing net that had these lead weights in it, I must have known I was going to do it because I had the lead weight in my pocket when I went into her building. I don't know why I went there, I was just driving around feeling the thing build up, the image, and when it got strong so I just couldn't stand it, then I'd just park and go into the first place coming along like it was just right for me to go in there. I went into number 77, I remember it said that on glass over the door in gold letters, and that the door was heavy but it was open and I just walked in. I went up to the top floor and she let me in without no trouble. Most of them was scared at first but I talk good and act like I don't care whether they let me in or not. I talk fast and I ain't sure what I'm saying sometimes, you know? Inside her apartment to the left was a kitchen then, down a little hall maybe ten feet, the bathroom. The light was on. I see a sewing machine. It was brown. A window with drapes, a light tan bedroom set, a couch, a record player, tan with darker colored knobs. The bathroom is yellow, the tub would be white and she was going to take a bath because there was water in it. Music is playing, long-hair symphonies and stuff like that, after I turned it off but I ain't sure if I got it all the way off. She took me along to show me the bathroom, what had to be done there for work, turning her back on me. When I see the back of her head I hit her on the head with the lead weight. She fell. I put my arm around her neck, and we fell together on the floor. She bleed a lot, terrible. After I put the belt around her neck I ripped open her robe and I played with her and pulled her legs apart, like this. I think she was still alive when I had intercourse with her. Then I look around and I'm angry, I don't know why and I don't really know what I'm looking for, you understand me? After, I took off my jacket and shirt and washed up and made a bundle. I grabbed her raincoat out of the brown cabinet in the bedroom. I went out wearing her raincoat, a tan one, carrying my shirt and jacket wrapped in my own raincoat. The first thing I see when I come out of the apartment is a cop. He looks at me but I don't pay no attention and go right past him to my car. I got into my car and drove around until I came to an army and navy store and I took off her raincoat and left it in the car and went into the store and bought a white shirt and put it on in the store. I drove towards Lynn and cut up my shirt and jacket with my fishing knife and threw them into a marsh where I know the waves will come and wash them away. Then I went home."

NINETEEN

ALBERT DESALVO WAS born in 1931 into a poor and violence-stunted family in the working-class city of Chelsea, which faces Boston across the foul waters of Chelsea Creek. There were oil terminals up Chelsea Creek, and tug-and-barge combos plowed past the Marginal Street wharves day and night pumping diesel exhaust up into the air. Al's father, Frank, was a drunk and a bully and a petty criminal who regularly brought prostitutes back to the apartment. The only quiet times in the DeSalvo household were when Frank was in jail. Al once saw his father punch his mother so hard that he knocked out most of her teeth. He also saw his father grab his mother's hand and bend her fingers back one by one until they broke. Frank regularly beat Albert and the other five children with a wide leather strap and once clubbed him with a length of pipe. When Albert was seven he had a sexual encounter with his older sister that was undoubtedly inspired by the father's wide-open displays with prostitutes. Frank DeSalvo appeared before judges on criminal charges eighteen times while Albert was growing up, five of them for assault against his wife. He was also brought in for larceny, breaking and entering, and nonpayment of child support.

Chelsea was a cramped little industrial city filled with people that Europe didn't want. The Irish came during the Great Potato Famine of the 1840s and established themselves by volunteering in huge numbers during the American Civil War. Every man who survived the war got a total of three hundred dollars, which many then used to start a small business in town. The Italians and the Poles came twenty years later, fleeing economic conditions that approached feudalism in their home countries. They were rough, uneducated people who were willing to work hard on the Chelsea waterfront and in the factories and freight businesses that sprang up in the postwar boom. The Jews came last, flushed out of Russia by a nationalistic frenzy instituted by Czar Alexander III in the 1880s. His ambition was to force Russia's Jews to convert, starve, or flee, and not surprisingly, many of them decided to flee. They arrived by the tens of thousands in New York and Boston and Chicago much the way blacks like Roy Smith arrived a generation or two later.

DeSalvo claimed that he was five when his father first taught him to shoplift, and he quickly moved up to theft, robbery, and breaking and entering. At age twelve he spent nearly a year in reform school for beating up a newspaper boy for the money in his pocket, and he returned to Chelsea to find his mother finally divorced from his father and living in a three-story brick tenement building at 353 Broadway. When young Albert leaned out his window he could look straight down Broadway to the Front Street wharves, and from the wharves he could see Charlestown across the harbor. Charlestown was run by Irish gangs, and if an Italian boy from Chelsea took the ferry over to Charlestown he would not come home looking the

same. In the other direction DeSalvo could look up Broadway to the
clamor and din of Bellingham Square and the Jewish-owned businesses clustered around city hall. His home was on the corner of
Fourth and Broadway. Across Fourth was a three-story building
known as the Goldberg Executive Building. It was constructed of
grim mustard-colored brick and ran the entire length of the block
toward Bellingham Square. There were small businesses on the
street level and a bank on the corner of Fourth and a movie theater
upstairs that was known as the Scratch Theater because a dime—
"scratch money"—would get a kid in all day.

The Executive Building was built in 1920 by a Russian Jew
named Simon Goldberg who had fled his home thirty years earlier
and settled in nearby Lawrence. He married a Chelsea woman of
similar background and had a son named Israel and a daughter
named Miriam, both of whom went to law school and became
lawyers. Israel, however, soon took over managing his father's prop-
erties, and after some ten or twenty years saved up enough money
to move to the quieter streets of Belmont. By then Israel had married a Chelsea woman named Bessie Koplevitz and had a young
daughter named Leah. He was known in Chelsea to wear an overcoat even when the weather was clear and to smoke a cigar and to
stand in the lobby of his theater on Saturdays to watch the people
come in for the show. DeSalvo must have passed him many times,
dime in hand, as he and the other children shuffled up the stairs and
in toward the cool darkness of the theater.

Every wave of immigrants to Chelsea brought with them not
only their particular brand of industry, but their particular brand of
crime, and by DeSalvo's time, Chelsea was awash in backroom hus-
tles and illicit cash. It was said that the Irish ran Chelsea but that the
Jews owned it. It was said that in Chelsea, a C-note would get you

anything you wanted. It was said that Chelsea was the most corrupt city in America. "I can't remember a time when I wasn't learning something I was better off not knowing," DeSalvo later told investigators about growing up there. Boston gangsters oversaw high-stakes dice games in Chelsea and old ladies ran numbers from corner stores and bartenders cashed checks for bookies who walked around with thousands of dollars in their pockets. The entire enterprise was overseen by a succession of corrupt mayors who financed their political campaigns by getting kickbacks from the thugs they were elected to protect. The corruption got so bad that when a fire burned much of West Chelsea in 1973, someone from the mayor's office tried to shake down a state telephone crew that had been sent to rehang the lines. The crew foreman tossed the mayor's man a hard hat from the back of a truck and told him to go back to city hall with that.

Despite its problems Chelsea remained in a prewar limbo of close neighborhoods and petty crime well into the sixties. There was a nighttime curfew for children—one of the few in the country—and paperboys had to dodge patrolmen in order to finish their routes in the morning. Middle-class families lived in graceful houses on Bellingham Hill, and everyone else was smashed into the neighborhoods of brick tenements and wood-frame triple-deckers that started a couple of blocks from the waterfront. There were acres of scrapyards in Chelsea, and iron foundries along Broadway, and lumberyards and varnish works on the waterfront, and Jewish rag shops that bought by the pound from old ragpickers who moved slowly through town on horse-drawn carts. When word came to Chelsea in 1963 that Israel Goldberg's wife, Bessie, had been murdered over in Belmont, old men on carts were still creaking down cobblestone streets in the poorer neighborhoods, calling out for rags.

The Poles and the Jews and the Italians and the Irish lived side by side in Chelsea without much trouble, and when violence happened it generally came from the outside. In 1963 a trio of small-time criminals drove into Chelsea, strode into the Goldberg Executive Building, and robbed the Lincoln National Bank. The police cornered them on Fourth Street, but they shot their way out, jumped into a car, and raced for the bridge out of town. The two who were caught immediately were arraigned in Chelsea District Court, where they faced a judge who happened to be president of the bank they had just robbed. Two years later a slope-eyed thug named Teddy Deegan was found shot to death in an alley behind the Goldberg building, having been lured there by several fellow gangsters who said they needed his help robbing a credit union on the second floor. The gangsters let Deegan walk into the alley first and then put two rounds in the back of his head and four in his chest.

The murder was the eleventh in a gang war that would see forty people dead before it was over, and the alley was immediately named "Deegan's Alley" in his honor. There were rumors that the men had then gone on to rob the credit union—and that Israel Goldberg was strongly advised to not report the matter—but that was never proved. One of Deegan's murderers, Joe "the Animal" Barboza, would go on to be an FBI informant, and when Barboza showed up on the initial Chelsea police investigation, the FBI stepped in to quash the arrest. The Chelsea police files disappeared almost immediately after the crime and did not turn up until 1998, when a construction worker found them buried beneath the police chief's floor.

DeSalvo grew up in Chelsea's odd blend of hard work and petty crime and quickly familiarized himself with both. He worked as a shoeshine boy and in a junk shop and on a pickle truck and spent his free time down along the waterfront looking for trouble and sex. From the waterfront he could look across Chelsea Creek at the flat-topped triple-deckers of East Boston. "There was always somebody to teach a boy over there about sex," DeSalvo told Bottomly about those years. "There was queers and funny old men and Greeks and older women who weren't getting what they wanted from grown men and they come around fooling with us kids. There was even a queer cop used to go under the piers. I used to swim a lot in the harbor in the summer, it was nice there in the water all alone with the city across the water and nobody to tell you what to do or how to do it. I used to shoot cats in the waterfront with a bow and arrow, put it right through their bellies, and sometimes they'd run away with the arrow right through them, yowling. Sometimes when I would see them, before the shot, I'd get such a feeling of anger that I think I could've torn those cats apart with my bare hands. I don't understand this. I don't usually hate cats or like them, either, for that matter. You understand me?"

The wharves provided refuge to the town's drunks and homeless and insane, and DeSalvo seemed to be able to hang out with them without getting drawn into their ruthless world. "There was kids there with no homes at all," he told John Bottomly. "That was where they lived, under the piers and in the old warehouses and wharves. They was wharf rats, that's what people called them and they was just like rats—I saw them roll a drunk one night, landing on him the way real rats would. They got that drunk down just like real rats and they practically tore him to pieces and then dumped the body into the water. We used to lie under a wharf near Maverick Square where the penny ferryboats came across from the Boston side and listen to the ship whistles in the harbor, funny, lonely sounds and the water slapping against the supports and the gulls out there sounding like cats."

At age fourteen DeSalvo stole a car and was sent to reform school. A few weeks into his sentence he escaped with two friends, but they were quickly tracked down and returned to custody. DeSalvo had to earn back three thousand demerit points even to be considered for parole. He got out the following year and returned to Chelsea, where he and his friends amused themselves by catching stray cats and dogs and starving them in boxes before releasing them to fight. The cats generally clawed the dogs' eyes out before the dogs managed to kill them. "The war was going on and there was a lot of sailors and soldiers around," DeSalvo told John Bottomly about those days. "We had a gang of kids used to hang around outside Arnie's Bar and Grill on First Street looking to roll these guys when they was too drunk to fight us kids off. I never was much for that stuff. I was a B&E [breaking-and-entering] man mostly, there was something exciting, thrilling about going into somebody's home. . . . I think now, too, that it had something to do with going into bedrooms where women had been sleeping or were sleeping and there was times when I would get a rail on just standing there outside the bedroom door listening to some woman breathe. It was only a matter of time before I would feel strong and tough enough to go into the bedroom when the woman was there alone and make her do what I wanted with her. But in those days I was a straight B&E man with a lot of sex on the side from the girls and the queers around the neighborhood. They . . . would pay for it, too, which was all right with me since I needed the dough and there was some relief from the urge that was pushing me to sex all the time, but it really was *woman* that I wanted, not any special one, just *woman*, with what a woman has."

DeSalvo made it to age seventeen without going to jail and—

much like Roy Smith—enlisted in the army as soon as he could. He trained in New Jersey and then was sent to Germany, where he was promoted to the rank of sergeant in the military police. He boxed his way to the army middleweight title in Europe despite having been injured when a shell misfired and exploded in the breech of a tank barrel. He met a young German woman named Irmgard Beck and eventually married her, but that did not prevent him from getting a lot of sex on the side. He claims he seduced the wives of American servicemen as well as German women who were just looking for a good time. He also pretended to be a scout for *Stars and Stripes* and would take the measurements of American nurses for what he called the "Best Sweetheart of All" contest. First prize was supposedly a trip to Italy. DeSalvo wasn't tall, but he was powerfully built and had a tough, handsome face and a surprising sweetness that many women must have imagined was especially for them.

Plenty of young men with violent fathers have gone on to lead turbulent lives, and DeSalvo was no exception. His troubles took a disturbing turn, though, when he was charged with carnal abuse of a young child in January 1955. He had been reassigned to Fort Dix, New Jersey, and was living there with his new wife, Irmgard. One afternoon he had knocked on the door of a private home in a nearby town and found himself talking to a nine-year-old girl whose mother had gone out to buy food for dinner. He told the girl he was looking for a house to rent, and the girl claimed he had then proceeded to put his hand on her chest and between her legs. He stopped and left the house only when the girl's younger brother wandered into the room. DeSalvo was picked up by the police because he was already under suspicion for entering another woman's house, and the girl positively identified him as the man who had touched her. The charges were eventually dropped because the girl's mother was reluctant to subject her daughter to the publicity of a trial.

After DeSalvo was honorably discharged from the military he moved back to Chelsea with Irmgard, got a series of low-paying jobs, and embarked on a breaking-and-entering spree that would see him arrested four times over the next year and a half. Every judge he faced gave him a suspended sentence. His luck finally ran out on March 17, 1961, when a Cambridge cop fired his revolver into the air and stopped DeSalvo in his tracks as he was fleeing an apartment building near Harvard University. The police put handcuffs on him and searched him and found a screwdriver, a skeleton key, and a jacknife in his pockets and four more screwdrivers in his car. DeSalvo's explanation for his situation was disarmingly innocent if disturbing: Yes, he'd tried to break into an apartment, but he hadn't intended to steal anything, he'd just wanted to surprise the two young nurses who lived there. How did he know that two nurses lived there? Well, a couple of weeks earlier, DeSalvo said he had knocked on their door and passed himself off as a scout for a modeling agency—his old *Stars and Stripes* routine. He'd asked the two women if they were interested in working as models and they said no, but he had remembered where they lived. And he had gone back.

The police were well aware of this scam. For months women had been calling the Cambridge police department to complain that a dark-haired young man named "Mr. Johnson" had knocked on their door and asked if they were interested in working as models. If they were, the man would pull a tape measure out of his pocket and measure all over their bodies—their legs, their waist, their bust—and then tell them that a representative from the "Black and

White Modeling Agency" would be in touch with them. Of course no one ever called.

Just the week before, a man by the same description had tried to break into another Cambridge apartment where two young women lived. It was a Saturday morning, and, hearing a tapping at the door, one of the women had opened it to find a strange man standing there stammering that he was an artist's agent. In fact, the tapping had been his attempts to jimmy the lock with a screwdriver. Are you a model? the man asked. When the young woman said no, the man tried to interest her in the idea. He finally left, saying that someone from the office would be in touch with her soon. The date was March 11, two years to the day before Bessie Goldberg was killed on Scott Road in Belmont. The question he asked was the same one that DeSalvo had asked my mother's young art student, Marie, before grabbing her around the waist and pulling her toward him.

The police had started referring to this intruder as the "Measuring Man," because he never attacked anyone, he just measured any woman who would let him. DeSalvo not only admitted to being the Measuring Man but boasted that some of these women had taken their clothes off so that their measurements would be smaller, and a few had even slept with him. "I'm not good-looking, I'm not educated, but I was able to put something over on high-class people," he explained. "They were college kids and I never had anything in my life and I outsmarted them." DeSalvo went on trial for assault and battery, for breaking and entering, and for lewdness and was convicted of the first two charges and acquitted of the third, which should have resulted in consecutive two-year sentences at the Middlesex House of Corrections. Judge Edward Viola first allowed DeSalvo to serve his sentences concurrently and then reduced them to eighteen months; the parole board ultimately let him out after ten.

THE POLICE HAD no cause to think about Albert DeSalvo for the next three years. Eleven women were strangled and sexually assaulted in Boston without his name ever coming up. DeSalvo got his job with Russ Blomerth and started working at my parents' house and did painting jobs on the side and by all accounts was a good husband and a hard worker and a decent neighbor. He and his family lived on a dead-end street in the working-class suburb of Malden, and the only tragedy in their life was a medical problem with their young daughter, Judy. She had been born with a hip deformity that threatened to cripple her for life, and the doctor fitted her with a brace and taught DeSalvo how to massage her. Every evening DeSalvo would place Judy on her back and unlace her brace and knead her thighs as hard as he could, and then tie the brace back up.

DeSalvo later claimed that his wife stopped having sex with him after Judy was born because she was terrified of having another deformed child. He even tried to get her to read the Kinsey Report so that she could see that his desire for sex was normal. Irmgard, for her part, told investigators that Al's sexual demands were so incessant that no woman could possibly have fulfilled them. Years later Al wrote Irmgard a six-page letter from prison explaining how much her rejection had hurt him. The letter is written longhand on notebook paper and is so filled with anguish that the sentences barely make sense. It reads, in part:

> I don't blame you for my troubles, but you will admit that if
> you treated me different like you told me all those years we

lost, the love I had been searching for, that we first had when we were married. Yes, Irm, I stole them. But why. What happened when Judy was born and we found out she may never walk. Irm from that day on you changed. All your love went to Judy. After I came out of jail—despite everything I tried to do—you denied me my rights as a husband. I am really and sincerely sorry for what I have done and will have to pay for it with years of my life. But apparently that is still not enough for you. You tell me not to write you or if I write you not to express in any way my love for you. So that even in this critical time when I need you most of all you are still making me feel hopeless. You can't [know] how awful it is to wait for letters that do not come. I will love you forever, always.

The year in jail DeSalvo referred to was his stint at the Middlesex House of Corrections after his Measuring Man escapades. He was released in April 1962, and apparently went home hoping that Irmgard would see his criminal behavior as a cry for help and change her own behavior accordingly. Judging by this letter, she didn't. If DeSalvo was indeed the Strangler, it may be significant that the murder of Anna Slesers happened two months after he got out of jail. She was the first woman to be killed, and it happened around the time that DeSalvo realized that nothing in his marriage had changed. According to him, at least, that was what had triggered his first, impulsive murder.

Al was known as a B&E man, not a sexual offender, so his name did not appear on a list of Strangler suspects until March 1965. By that time he was already back in prison for a series of sexual attacks in the Boston area. He'd been picked up the previous November because he strongly resembled a police sketch of a man who had appeared unexpectedly one morning in the bedroom of a young Cambridge woman. The man wore aviator glasses and a dark waist-length jacket and green pants and his hair was stylishly combed back with grease, and he put a knife to the young woman's throat and tied her to the bed and commenced to molest her. Before he got very far, however, he seemed to have second thoughts and asked the woman how to leave her apartment. And then he was gone.

A detective who saw the sketch thought it looked like the old Measuring Man, and Cambridge asked police in Malden to bring DeSalvo in for questioning. He was put in a lineup and immediately picked out by the woman who had been attacked, who recognized his voice as well. The police knew of three other women who had been attacked in a similar way, including an old lady who managed to give DeSalvo pause by demanding to know what his mother would think of his activities. She wouldn't like it, DeSalvo admitted before mas-turbating in front of her and leaving.

None of these four women had been raped or seriously molested, and again, the timing of this may be significant. In his let-ter to Irmgard, DeSalvo added a postscript that said, in part: "Our last two months together you made me feel for the first time like a man. You gave me love I never dreamed you had to give." The two months he referred to were September and October 1965, immedi-ately before he was arrested. If DeSalvo was indeed the Boston Strangler, as he claimed, the timing would make sense. According to him he killed because of rage at his wife, and now that things were better at home, he could continue his lifelong compulsion of break-ing into women's homes and still catch himself before things got out of hand. He even apologized to one woman as he left.

DeSalvo was arraigned and again charged with B&E, assault and battery, and engaging in unnatural and lascivious acts, though this time the court added confining and putting in fear because he had tied his victims up. He was released on eight thousand dollars' bail, but was rearrested almost immediately because his photograph— which had gone out by teletype to police departments across New England—matched descriptions of a man who was wanted by the state police in Connecticut. Maybe DeSalvo hadn't raped anyone in Massachusetts, but the previous spring and summer a man who looked exactly like him had raped dozens of women in other New England states—including four women in one morning in the Hartford–New Haven area. In almost every case a dark-haired man wearing green cotton work pants had broken into a woman's home, tied her to her bed, and then raped her. None of the women were killed. Because of his clothes the rapist was known in Connecticut as the "Green Man." Women who were shown the teletype photograph of DeSalvo said they were absolutely sure that he was the man who had attacked them.

DeSalvo now had out-of-state warrants against him and a bail of one hundred thousand dollars. He was sent to Bridgewater State Hospital for pretrial observation and was quickly diagnosed with "sociopathic personality disorder marked by sexual deviation, with promi-nent schizoid features and depressive trends." His mental health appeared to deteriorate over the next couple of months, and at his pretrial hearing the judge ruled that he was incompetent to stand trial and sent him back to Bridgewater indefinitely. The date was February 4, 1965.

One month later DeSalvo met with a well-known lawyer named F. Lee Bailey and spent an hour in an interview room trying to prove that he, Albert DeSalvo, was in fact the Boston Strangler. Bailey took the information and went straight to Ed Brooke, state attorney general.

TWENTY

ALBERT DESALVO, Bridgewater Correctional Institution: "Well, I been riding around all day like in the middle of the world and I got to this parking lot down on Commonwealth Avenue and I left my car there and I walked to number 1940. It was awful hot and I could feel the sweat on me and smell it, too, and I don't like that because I like to keep my body very clean. I look at the names on the mailboxes and the bells inside number 1940 and pick out a couple of women's names and press the first one. I stand there waiting, feeling the image build up and not thinking about what I'm going to say to her because I know something will come to me like it always does. Nothing happens. I press the second doorbell and in a few minutes she buzzes the door, twice, and I walk into the hallway. The stairs are curved around an elevator and to the right and I go up them, not in a hurry or nothing, just taking them one at a time. Its funny, isn't it, how the first woman didn't answer the bell or wasn't home or something and just that little chance, you understand what I mean?

"She had on a robe, you might say a housecoat, the color was reddish to me, pinkish. She was wearing glasses and blue sneakers, I remember that, don't I? What do you want, she said, and she sounded kind of mad, kind of impatient, as if I was a bother to her. I said, 'We been wanting to check your apartment for leaks.' It always came to me what to say and it was always something simple and easy and that could happen natural, you know? And she said, 'Oh, all right, come in but make it fast I'm just getting ready to go out.' But I already know she aint going nowhere after I close that door behind me even though I fight it all the way. It's funny, I didn't want to go in there in the first place I just didn't want it to happen. I go in and go from one room to the other with her. In the bedroom she turned her back on me and I see the back of her head and I was all hot, just like my head was going to blow off as soon as I saw the back of her head, not her face. I got her from behind and both her and I fell backward on the bed. Now I am not telling this as it happened. I don't like to talk about this. I grabbed her and she fell back with me on the bed, on top of me. We just missed one of the bedposts, I guess you call them, and I was in this position—here, you see, my arms around her neck and my feet around the bottom of her legs, do you understand?

"This is very hard and I'm sorry to be mixed up like this but what come later was something I don't like to talk about, you understand me? I mean about the bottle and her privates—what was the word you said?—yes, that and her lying there and the thing with the bottle, you know? That's very hard for me. I thought I remembered at first she had shoes on, she may have had shoes on or house slippers or something on. Just until now I wasn't sure about that. I'm trying to respond to your questions, sir, in a way that will make it all clear to and help me to clean myself inside which is what I wish to do and I answer, yes, as she fell she fell back on top of me and she was still conscious and I took her off the bed and I don't know, did I put her on the floor? I would say that I lied her on the floor, I don't know if it was a wooden floor or if it had a rug on there, and I opened her housecoat, tearing some of the buttons and she was wearing something underneath. I believe that it was at least a bra and panties and that I lifted them off—no it was just a slip and I lifted it above her waist and I had intercourse with her there in the floor and for a minute I felt good and then I looked at her and she still looked alive and so I went and got two nylon stockings, I put a silk stocking around her neck and knotted it, tight, three times like this and all the time the thing is building up in me again and I'm getting mad, very angry as I look at her there without her glasses on and her eyes wide open which she might be dead or not but she aint moving and it gets me mad, very very angry to see her like that so I take another silk stocking and put it around her neck, hooking it and twisting it with the other one and knotting it and pulling them so tight that they cut into her neck and I know she aint about to breathe no more."

TWENTY-ONE

DESALVO TOLD BAILEY that he wanted to confess to thirteen murders in exchange for immunity from prosecution and transfer to a medical facility where he could get treatment for his psychological problems. He also wanted to sell the book rights to his story so that he could support his family from prison. Over the next several months DeSalvo submitted to an interrogation under hypnosis and recorded fifty hours of detailed confessions for John Bottomly, head of the Strangler Bureau. The transcripts were eventually released to the public in the form of highly processed excerpts in a book called *Confessions of the Boston Strangler*, by George William Rae. In the first chapter of his book, Rae explains to his readers that in order to protect DeSalvo's legal rights, the words attributed to him "are not presented as legally exact quotations—although they come from impeccable sources and follow closely his intellectual and grammatical formulations."

Rae altered DeSalvo's testimony to give him some legal protec-

tions, but there is no reason to believe—and no one has ever suggested—that he invented anything outright. Compressed into the
kind of smooth-flowing narrative that Rae created, the tapes certainly did seem to provide an abundance of information that only a
killer could know. The raw transcripts tell a different story, however.
In them DeSalvo's descriptions of the murders are clumsy and halt-
ing, and he often gropes his way through the details only with the
help of John Bottomly, who breaks with accepted procedure and
keeps hinting at the right answers.

Doubts about DeSalvo's confession arose almost immediately.
Not only did many cops dismiss DeSalvo as a braggart and a punk,
but they deeply resented the fact that John Bottomly had been
handed the Strangler Bureau without any experience in criminal
investigation. To make matters worse, any number of important
people had something to gain from a successful conclusion to the
Strangler investigation, and that fact alone cast doubt on virtually
everything that DeSalvo said. Bottomly could clear the entire slate
of murders and disband the Strangler Bureau, which would be a
tremendous boon to his political career. Attorney General Ed
Brooke could make good use of the success in his upcoming senate
campaign. F. Lee Bailey could take credit for yet another high-profile
case. And Albert DeSalvo—already facing life in prison for serial
rape—could sell the rights to his story and become a star in his own
psychological drama.

Certainly jailhouse confessions are a dubious proposition. Of the
two hundred or so convicted murderers in this country who have
been released from prison because they were later proved to be
innocent, one out of five confessed to the crime. The interrogation
process can be so coercive, in other words, that innocent and guilty
alike cooperate simply to put an end to their misery. And DeSalvo

wasn't a run-of-the-mill criminal; he was a high-profile rapist who had every reason to cooperate. Comfortably settled in prison with a high-profile lawyer and a flourishing drug racket, DeSalvo stood to reap huge financial benefits from movie and book deals by claiming to be the Boston Strangler. But the fact that he—or anyone else—stood to gain does not, in and of itself, prove that his confessions are false. The people who thought so were falling for a classic logical fallacy known as "asserting the consequent." Rain makes the ground wet, but wet ground doesn't prove it has rained; someone could just have turned on the sprinkler. Likewise with DeSalvo: The fact that some murder suspects falsely confess in exchange for movie deals doesn't mean that every suspect with a movie deal has falsely confessed; guilty men like movie deals as well.

The other main reason people doubted DeSalvo's confessions were the numerous errors and blank spots in his memory. The extent of these errors was not commonly known until 1995, when a journalist named Susan Kelly reexamined transcripts of the original confessions in a book called *The Boston Stranglers*. According to Kelly's thoroughly researched book, much of DeSalvo's confessions was wrong, and the parts that weren't wrong could easily have come from newspaper accounts and prompting by John Bottomly. Every murder had these errors. When questioned by Bottomly about Anna Slesers, for example, DeSalvo could not easily remember the color of the lining of her housecoat, whether there was a wastebasket in her bedroom, or what kind of music was playing on her phonograph. And there were more significant errors as well: He could not remember the date Nina Nichols was killed—even though it had appeared in the newspapers. He could not remember her street address. He could not remember what floor she lived on. He said he raped Helen Blake when in fact she was not raped; he said he raped Ida Irga when in fact she was not raped; he said he raped Mary Sullivan when in fact she was not raped.

On and on the list went, thirteen murders half remembered by a man who claimed he'd committed them but who mainly seemed able to recite details that had already appeared in the papers. Even more damning, some of the facts that he got wrong were also reported incorrectly in the newspapers. It looked, in other words, as though DeSalvo had just studied the newspaper accounts and absorbed everything, correct or otherwise. Kelly's explanation for DeSalvo's errors was that he was lying, and that's certainly a possibility. But it's not the *only* possibility. Perfect recall by criminals— by anyone—does not exist, and exceptionally violent incidents are known to trigger temporary amnesia not only in eyewitnesses but in the perpetrators as well. Sirhan Sirhan readily admitted killing Robert Kennedy in the Ambassador Hotel in 1968, but he remembered almost nothing of how he had done it. Soldiers who have won the Medal of Honor for heroism during combat typically remember very little of the incident that won them the medal. Furthermore, murderers read the newspapers like everyone else, so not only correct details but *incorrect* ones as well could conceivably work their way into a confused killer's memory. DeSalvo, in fact, told John Bottomly that one of the reasons he remembered the names of his victims was because he read them in the newspaper the next day.

In 1984 in Annapolis, Maryland, a teenage boy named Larry Swartz had a brief, unpleasant exchange with his foster mother and then shocked himself by suddenly grabbing a ten-pound splitting maul and burying it in the back of her head. He went on to kill his father with a knife before going to bed and then called 911 in the morning. Swartz eventually confessed to the police, but his memory was highly distorted by the sheer violence of the scene. He remembered growling like a dog while he was doing the killing and also remembered looking down from the ceiling as if watching someone else. His memories were fractured and distorted and significantly inconsistent with the evidence. Those memories, however, may well show what murder looks like through the eyes of a murderer.

"He told me his body was working very quickly, his mind was working very slowly," Swartz's lawyer explained to a local reporter. "He would see himself stab [his mother] in the throat. His mind would somehow say, 'God, you've got to stop that!' But by the time the thought had formed, he would see himself stabbing her again. He described it to me as, 'My mind never caught up with my body.' Then he turned around and saw his father standing there on the landing with what he called a blank look. He heard himself growl like a wolf or a dog and realized it was himself. He sensed himself taking one giant step and his father fell back into the computer room. He recalls his father trying to shut the door and Larry just brushing it aside. Larry told me it was like the door wasn't even there."

The psychological term for this is "dissociation"; it is an adaptive mechanism that allows people who are undergoing extreme trauma—either killers or victims—to insulate themselves from reality. Dissociation does not open the door to violence; rather, it is triggered by the first puzzling blow. After that both killer and victim find themselves in a slow-motion dream that neither can escape. It is an odd and sluggish dream where the inner narration in the mind of the killer—"I can't believe I'm strangling this woman"— is roughly mirrored by the inner narration of the victim, who is thinking, "I can't believe this man is actually strangling me." Victims of near-fatal car accidents often dissociate, as do people who survive falls from great heights or are attacked by wild animals. Time slows down in a dissociative state. There is a sense of unreality, as if what is happening has to be a dream. Certain details become very vivid, and others are completely wiped out. In Swartz's case he hit his mother with the splitting maul and then had a memory of her breathing so loudly that he felt compelled to make it stop by cutting her throat with a knife. In reality his mother was so badly wounded that her breathing must have been nearly inaudible, but Larry Swartz's mind fixated on it to the point where it overwhelmed every other sound in the room.

After the murders Swartz regained his senses enough to try to hide the evidence, but police easily linked him to the crime. When he finally gave his confession, he sobbed so violently that he could barely speak. He spent hours with the police trying to reconstruct what had happened that night, but his memory never matched the evidence that was found at the scene. The most puzzling of these inconsistencies were shoeless footprints in the snow that left the Swartz house and meandered half a mile around the neighborhood before returning home. Larry Swartz was the only person who could have left those tracks, but he had no memory of it. All he had was an unexplained gash on one foot and a dim recollection of a "burning sensation"—because his feet were frozen?—at some point after the murders.

If Swartz could run a half mile barefoot through the snow and not remember it the next day, DeSalvo could forget the color of Anna Slesers's housecoat or even the exact manner of her violation. DeSalvo took credit for thirteen murders in all, including the brutal clubbing death of Mary Brown several days before Bessie Goldberg's murder, and the death by heart attack of an elderly woman who caught him breaking into her apartment. Neither the clubbing death nor the heart attack had been considered "Boston

Stranglings," and yet he had claimed them anyway. The amount of raw information in even the most cursory newspaper articles was enormous, on the order of fifteen or twenty core facts for each murder. And there was probably an equal number of lesser details—the color of Nina Nichols's housecoat, for example—that would never have made it into the papers. Had DeSalvo not killed anyone, he would have had to memorize as many as five hundred random facts about the murders, a sort of grim trivia contest. But what would constitute a "high" or a "low" score in such a contest? If DeSalvo got, say, *half* the details correct, was that a lot or a little?

Put another way, if a man went on blind dates with thirteen different women and was asked years later what the women had worn the night he took them out, what they'd ordered for dinner, what music was playing, and what the waiter looked like, would a score of 50 percent be reasonable? Ten percent? These were not dates, though, they were murders, and killers who dissociate tend to fixate on certain details of their crimes and block out others. That could make a culprit's testimony both very compelling and very spotty. DeSalvo's testimony, if true, pointed strongly toward some degree of dissociation.

"When it turned, it did it fast," he told Bottomly about his sudden slide into violence. "I was only angry at two of the Strangler's women, both of them had said something to me that made me angry. The rest of them, I don't know, I just found myself doing it to them . . . either in a daze or like a dream or standing there watching myself do it. And sometimes after, I would not think it was me with my arm around the old woman's neck, or me with my hand on a woman's throat and she hadn't done nothing to me, in fact she'd been very good to me. All I know is that something would happen and I would have my arms around their necks."

TWENTY-TWO

I T WAS ONLY a matter of time before someone remembered
Bessie Goldberg. DeSalvo never mentioned her name, but the
murder was almost identical to many others that he confessed
to, and those confessions were filled with references to Belmont.
Any alert investigator would eventually get around to wondering
whether there was some connection between the two. My mother,
like a lot of people, always thought that Roy Smith might be innocent, so she was not surprised when a detective from the Strangler
Bureau called and asked if she would answer some questions
about Albert DeSalvo. Sometime in early 1966, Lt. Andrew Tuney
and Detective Steve Delaney drove out to Belmont, parked in
front of our house at 21 Cedar Road, and walked up the brick path
to our door.

Delaney was not new to the Goldberg murder. Two years earlier,
just after he'd started working at the Strangler Bureau, Attorney
General Ed Brooke had stopped by his desk to ask a favor.
Delaney's job was to read through the crates of files, looking for

patterns to the murders, and Brooke wanted him to add the Goldberg murder to the list. Were there similarities, Brooke wanted to know, between the modus operandi of the Goldberg murder and the other murders?

It was a politically risky request because Smith had already been convicted—in fact his case was currently under appeal—and Brooke was essentially suggesting that someone else might have committed the murder. If the press found out, they would have a field day with it. A couple of weeks later Brooke ran across Delaney in the office and asked him if he'd had time to go through the Goldberg file. Delaney told him that he had, and that the MO had seemed to him exactly the same.

Brooke said he was sorry to hear that—very sorry—because word had gotten out that the Strangler Bureau was still investigating the Goldberg murder and it had turned into a political bombshell. Delaney would have to give the file back. According to Delaney, the Middlesex district attorney had gone to the State Supreme Court and complained that the attorney general's office could not simultaneously review the Roy Smith verdict and also explore the possibility that someone else had committed the murder. It was a conflict of interest. The judges agreed and ordered Brooke to reclaim the file from Delaney.

Still, Delaney had seen enough for him to have serious doubts about Smith's guilt. Even though he was young, he had already seen so much rule bending in the system—by everyone from beat cops to county prosecutors—that he took nothing for granted. Such skepticism about the criminal justice system is rare in a cop, and it's probably no coincidence that soon thereafter, he quit the police force and went on to work as an investigator for F. Lee Bailey. Decades later, he found work helping to overturn bogus rape and murder convictions with a legal aid group in New Jersey called Centurion Ministries. The misconduct that Centurion has uncovered is staggering. One prosecutor they investigated secretly paid his main witness seventy thousand dollars in exchange for crucial testimony. Another prosecutor sent a man named Jimmy Wingo to the electric chair with the unsupported testimony of a lone witness who had lied under oath. She lied, Centurion discovered, because a deputy sheriff had threatened to take her children away if she didn't; he also coerced her into sleeping with him. In yet another case, an innocent man got a life sentence only because the prosecutor relentlessly pressured three uncooperative witnesses to lie in court. "I will eat stone," the man told the court after being found guilty. "I will eat dust. I will eat anything . . . to prove my innocence. I am not the man." Centurion eventually got the case overturned and was commended by a higher court for their work.

That phase of Delaney's life was still decades in his future, but when he and Andy Tuney drove out to Belmont to talk to my mother, he was already a young man keenly attuned to the idea of injustice. Tuney did not necessarily share Delaney's idealism—or cynicism, depending on how you looked at it—but he was a seasoned investigator who could be counted on to do a thorough job. He had already talked to Russ Blomerth about the kind of worker DeSalvo was. "Couldn't get him mad," Tuney had written in his notes about DeSalvo. "Never got tired. Very strong. Unbelievable strength. Didn't show any great interest re: stranglings." Blomerth said that DeSalvo had come recommended by a man named Andy Amerault, who had worked with DeSalvo at the Monroe Shipyards. Blomerth hired him on September 4, 1962, a few days after the fifth strangling in Boston, and let him go the following August. In that time Blomerth said that DeSalvo worked briefly on another job in

Belmont and then moved on to my parents' house. He worked roughly forty hours a week but had no set schedule and occasionally spent time on his own. On February 18—the date that Erika Wilsing was attacked in her apartment—DeSalvo was not on the clock for Russ Blomerth. On March 4 and 5—two of the possible dates for the murder of Mary Brown in Lawrence—DeSalvo was also not on the clock. He worked at my parents' house Wednesday, March 6, and Thursday, March 7, and then returned the following Monday. That was the day Bessie Goldberg was killed.

At the knock my mother opened the front door, let the two detectives into the living room, and offered them a seat on the couch. Tuney was a tall, attention-getting man who was already a grandfather at forty-three but still managed to maintain a certain reputation around town. ("Good booze and bad broads is what keeps us going," he once told a newspaper reporter about detective work.) Delaney was recently separated from his wife and trying to decide whether or not to continue police work. My mother brought out a calendar with the dates of the studio job marked on it and described the incident in the basement and the incident with her student, Marie. She showed them the photograph of her and Al and me and pointed out the ladder in the background that Al had been standing on when she told him about the Goldberg murder.

My mother wanted to know what would have happened if she had gone down into the basement. The detectives agreed that DeSalvo wouldn't have dared kill her, but they said he might have attempted a very forceful seduction. If he had killed her, they reasoned, he immediately would have become a suspect, and he was too smart for that. Delaney asked if he could keep the calendar and my mother said that that would be all right, and after half an hour or so the men got up and put on their coats and hats and said good-

bye. Either that same day or the next—Delaney doesn't remember—the two men marked their car odometer in front of my parents' house and then drove through Belmont to Scott Road. The
distance was 1.2 miles.

Was it possible? Could DeSalvo have gotten into his car, driven
to Scott Road, knocked on Bessie Goldberg's door, talked his way in,
raped her, killed her, and then gotten back to our house before my
mother and I arrived home? The trickiest—or least likely—part of
this scenario was on Scott Road, where DeSalvo would have had to
slip unnoticed past the neighborhood children. He also would have
had to get into and out of the Goldberg house during the forty-
eight-minute window between Roy Smith's departure and Israel
Goldberg's arrival. He would be threading an awfully small needle
to do it, but it was still possible.

Another problem was the location: According to the FBI's analysis, all the murders DeSalvo claimed to have committed were in
apartment buildings where many people came and went and resi-
dents might not be surprised if a maintenance man knocked on
their door. But this was a house in the suburbs where a stranger
would stand out immediately because everyone on the street knew
one another by their first names. Once you have DeSalvo in the
house the crime is pure Boston Strangler, but how do you get him
there? And why would a killer who claimed to have developed such
a perfect technique for killing women suddenly abandon it for
something far riskier?

Tuney and Delaney parked on Scott Road and walked around
the Goldberg house, noting where the front and back doors were
and how far Smith had to walk to get to the bus stop on Pleasant
Street. One of the first things that struck Delaney was that the
Goldberg house was easily approached from the back; it was a route,

in fact, that neighborhood children said they used as a shortcut. If a killer wanted to enter the Goldberg house unseen from Scott Road, all he had to do was cross behind the Hartunians' house on the corner of Pleasant Street and walk about 120 feet to the Goldbergs' backyard. Workmen would not ordinarily use the front door of a house like the Goldbergs', so Bessie might not be suspicious if a man knocked on her kitchen door and said, for example, that he worked for the Belmont Water Department and wanted to check her meter.

But even that maneuver might not have been necessary. Beryl Cohen didn't emphasize this at trial, but the children of Scott Road played in front of the Goldberg home for only part of the time that Bessie was supposedly alone inside. Roy Smith left the house shortly after three o'clock, right around the time that Dougie Dreyer, Myrna Spector, and Melissa Lovett were walking up Pleasant Street and approaching the corner of Scott Road. They remembered passing Smith on the corner, and they remembered that he seemed in a hurry. The children went to their respective homes, and Dougie told the Belmont police that he didn't go back outside again until 3:25, which was when the school bus usually dropped Susan Faunce off at the corner. When Dougie went back out onto the street, he saw Susan standing in front of Myrna Spector's house talking to her through an open window. The time was 3:30 p.m. From that moment on, the neighborhood children were playing kickball directly in front of the Goldberg house until Israel came home, and anyone who wanted to enter or exit unnoticed would have had to do it through the back. No one, however, was watching the Goldberg house from 3:05 to 3:25. That did not mean that Smith was innocent, but it certainly made it less sure that he was guilty.

If Delaney was the idealist of the two, Tuney was the seasoned pragmatist. He'd been in police work long enough to know that the politics of a case are everything, and that if you ignore them you'll get nowhere. Consequently, the first thing he'd done on the way to Scott Road was to stop at the Belmont police department and let the police chief know they were in the area. It wasn't required but it was a matter of respect, and it may have been a courtesy that paid off. Delaney is not positive where they got this information, but he believes it was from someone at the Belmont police department. Apparently a neighbor of the Goldbergs' had seen a suspicious person on Scott Road on the afternoon of the murder and had called the Belmont police with the information, but they had not followed up on it. The lead, such as it was, now belonged to Tuney and Delaney.

The neighbor turned out to be an elderly man with a bedridden wife, and Delaney has a memory of standing back while Tuney asked the man to repeat his story. On the afternoon that Bessie Goldberg was killed, the neighbor said, he'd been approached by a man in work clothes who had offered to paint his house as a side job on weekends. The man was white and probably in his thirties and—in Delaney's mind, at least—roughly matched a description of DeSalvo. The old man said he declined the work offer by saying that a private nurse he'd hired to help his wife needed him back in the house. The incident had stuck in his mind, though, and an hour later—when he saw police cars and an ambulance on Scott Road—he'd called the police department.

By then, however, every cop in Massachusetts was already looking for Roy Smith, and a white man walking around a white neighborhood knocking on doors would have meant absolutely nothing. That was, however, something that DeSalvo said he often did to find weekend work. Maybe he knocked on Goldberg's door and Bessie opened, Delaney thought. Maybe she let him in. Maybe he said he needed to check her water meter or offered to paint her living room. Maybe she just turned away for a moment and he was on her. It was a classic Boston Strangling except that DeSalvo never confessed to it and Roy Smith was convicted of it; in every other respect it was identical to the thirteen murders he claimed to have committed.

Delaney and Tuney finished up on Scott Road and drove back to Boston without anything concrete to report. It was a delicate line of inquiry anyway—what with Smith's case under appeal and the attorney general himself warned away from making any awkward comparisons to other murders. It was a case, however, that Delaney never managed to get out of his head.

TWENTY-THREE

GEORGE NASSAR, MCI–Cedar Junction (formerly Walpole State Prison):

"Al's reason for killing his victims was so they wouldn't be witnesses. It was a rational criminal decision because he had already been convicted on eyewitness testimony. His first victim he had in a stranglehold, and it happened to be in her bedroom, and there was a large mirror, and he saw himself strangling her and he stopped. He made sure never to do it in front of a mirror again. When he had a stranglehold on a woman he would block her carotid artery. He did it to me once, he was playing with me one day and he put his thumb and forefinger on the carotid artery and I nearly passed out—it was only a matter of seconds. Once he got you in that stranglehold, one arm became the fulcrum for the other hand, and then he'd fall backward onto the floor. After the other person lost consciousness, only *then* would he apply the ligature. He said his sex urges would come over him suddenly and uncontrollably; he'd be walking down the street, and it would just come over him. It was not the woman herself, it was the opportunity. If the situation—not her—looked good, he acted. It was truly the free floating of the diabolic."

Nassar met DeSalvo in 1965 at MCI-Bridgewater, where they were both being evaluated by a state psychologist to determine if they were legally sane. DeSalvo was awaiting trial for four sexual assaults around Boston, and Nassar had been charged with shooting and stabbing a gas station attendant during a holdup in Andover, Massachusetts. He was also charged with trying to kill a woman and her fourteen-year-old daughter who had witnessed the murder; they survived only because the gun misfired. Nassar, now four decades into a life sentence, plays chess and speaks Russian and reads dictionaries and is rumored to have an IQ in excess of 150. It has also been reported that he is a diagnosed schizophrenic and sociopath with zero empathy for others.

"Al was insistent that Wiggins was the most important and fondly regarded male figure of his life," says Nassar, referring to the old master carpenter on Blomerth's crew. "Al was so repetitive and mawkish about it that I was cloyed by it. I remember he either wanted to, tried to, or succeeded in a contact—through his brother, I think—after his exposure. And he seemed to hope beyond hope that Wiggins's wife, as I understood it, would still be warm to him. So I'm reconfirmed that that man and woman were his ideal surrogate parents, and now that I see the photo you sent, that that woman and her child would be ideally Al's wife and son."

The photograph Nassar was referring to was the one that Blomerth took in the studio the day before the job was finished. Floyd Wiggins, who lived near DeSalvo in Malden, stands off his right shoulder with a claw hammer shoved in his front pocket. My mother and I are sitting in front of the two men. If Nassar is correct, that photograph represents DeSalvo's life as it could have been: A

gentle father, a loving wife, a healthy child. Instead, DeSalvo got a
father who was a violent drunk, a wife who refused to have sex with
him, and a daughter who was crippled from birth. That, DeSalvo
told Nassar, was why his life had gone so wrong; that was why he
was driven to kill.

Now he was facing hard time in prison, and the only thing he
had going for him was an explosive secret—or lie—about his past.
Nassar was savvy about the world in a way that DeSalvo was not,
and DeSalvo eventually turned to him for advice. Could a man who
claimed to be the Strangler, he wanted to know, make a lot of
money off book and movie rights to his life story? Nassar said he'd
find out, and the next time he saw F. Lee Bailey, his lawyer, he put
the question to him. Bailey said that a man who confessed to being
the Boston Strangler would go straight to the electric chair, movie
deal or no movie deal, unless he had first-rate legal representation.
Within days Bailey was sitting down with DeSalvo in a visiting
room in Bridgewater State Prison.

True or not, DeSalvo's confessions promised to pay everyone
quite well. DeSalvo hoped to collect hundreds of thousands of dollars from book, magazine, and movie deals, which he would then
use to support his family. Bailey would be paid off for his services
from what was left over. And George Nassar would attempt to collect reward money that had been offered by the governor of the
state. The idea that a murderer, a rapist, and a high-profile lawyer
were going to make enormous amounts of money on a series of
gruesome sex murders was bound to arouse suspicion, however,
and a rumor started that Nassar was the real Boston Strangler. He
supposedly spent his time in Bridgewater tutoring DeSalvo in the
details of the crimes, and DeSalvo retained almost all of it because
he was thought to have a "photographic" memory.

This theory was particularly popular in the Cambridge police department, which had always chafed under the authority of the attorney general's office. Cambridge believed that the one murder that happened in their jurisdiction—Beverly Samans, in early May 1963, was an independent incident, and it infuriated them that Ed Brooke's Strangler Bureau had come in and just taken it over. What these rumors about Nassar did not address, however, was whether a man who was capable of one kind of violence would be predisposed toward another. Nassar was twice convicted of murdering men in cold blood, but there was absolutely no sexual violence in his past. It was not at all clear that Nassar's apparent willingness to shoot a man in the chest during a robbery would make him, psychologically, a more likely candidate for raping and strangling old women. DeSalvo's past, by contrast, was a textbook case of how sex offenders are created. He grew up in an extremely violent household, he was exposed to deviant sex at a very young age, and he went on to develop a voyeuristic obsession with women that quickly escalated to assault and rape. None of this proved he was the Boston Strangler, but it certainly made him a good candidate.

And it also made for a great insanity defense. In January 1967 DeSalvo was put on trial for what were known as his "Green Man" crimes—his rapes and sexual assaults in Massachusetts—and out of DeSalvo's sordid past Bailey devised an odd and ingenious strategy. DeSalvo was innocent, Bailey would argue, because he was driven to commit his crimes by an "irresistible impulse," which was the core of any insanity defense. The proof of that impulse, according to Bailey, was that he had murdered thirteen women, but DeSalvo could not be prosecuted for those crimes because he had confessed under condition of immunity. Bailey, in other words, wanted to use testimony that was beyond the reach of the law to reach back *into* the law and exonerate his client. During a pretrial hearing, Bailey put DeSalvo on the stand and asked him whether he understood that he could be given a life sentence. DeSalvo said that he did.

"Mr. DeSalvo," Bailey said. "Is it your purpose in this trial to deny the commission of these offenses?"

"No, sir, it isn't," DeSalvo answered.

"And do you understand what defense will be raised in your behalf?"

"Yes, sir."

"What will that be? Can you tell the court?"

"For the purpose that I hired you in the first place: Not to deny these charges but to somehow explain the truth and tell the truth of all this happening. I would like to know myself why all this took place."

To give some backbone to his insanity defense, Bailey brought in a renowned psychologist named Dr. James Brussel, who had helped solve a famous serial bomber case case in New York City in the 1950s. Brussel had already seen service on the Strangler Bureau and was one of the few psychologists who thought that the stranglings were the work of one man. He had interviewed DeSalvo in depth about his compulsion to murder, and under direct examination by Bailey, he repeated what he'd heard.

"It would start the night before with a burning up inside, like little fires, little explosions," Brussel testified. "And he would get up in the morning feeling hungry, yet he would not eat and he did not want to eat. And he would get in his car or truck and drive, sometimes not knowing where he was going, and on occasion he would suddenly look around and find that he was in Connecticut or Rhode Island and ask himself, What am I doing here? He would drive to an apartment house or a multiple dwelling that he knew, and he would go inside. He would indiscriminately punch doorbell keys until he got an answer, and then he would go into the apartment and he would say that he had been sent by the super to repair a leak or to fix up some painting. It would be early morning frequently, and the woman who answered the door would be variously dressed in sleeping attire or a robe. Once her back was turned to him, the indescribable compulsion, as he put it to me—the feeling of hatred, the hatred of his wife having turned her back on him, the feeling that he was not being shown affection, which his mother had never shown him—simply swept over him. And these little fires and these little explosions within would mount to a pitch where he would . . . quickly use one arm around the neck."

When the jury looked over, DeSalvo was sobbing quietly in the jury box. It was either great testimony or great theater, but the prosecutor, Donald Conn of the Middlesex DA's office, would have none of it. Conn was a classmate of Bailey's from Boston University, and he had a bold, aggressive style that made him well suited to the high stakes of the case. "This is a man who is going to turn certain conduct in his history into one million dollars!" Conn thundered at the jury during his summation. "Are you going to sit and acquit this man? You are going to have to live with your conscience when you leave here. You have a duty . . . to your wife, to my wife, to everyone who could conceivably be the subject of an attack of this type. And not to be manipulated and not to have a man come here and feign and fake symptoms and con you right out of this box."

The jury retired to deliberate. Three hours and forty-five minutes later they filed back into the courtroom and the jury foreman, a brokerage-firm analyst named F. Hunter Rowley, declared that they had found DeSalvo guilty of all ten charges against him. Judge Cornelius Moynihan asked Bailey whether he had anything to say concerning the sentencing, and Bailey stood and said that he did.

Bailey was an impressive-looking man who wore expensive suits and sported a gold pocket watch on a thin gold chain. His office, according to one reporter, was littered with full ashtrays and empty whiskey bottles and was run by a tall brunette named Terri, who had both a pilot's license and a Harvard Law degree.

"The evidence has made clear the defendant's desire to remain in a situation where society is protected from him," Bailey told Judge Moynihan. "And I think if I were sitting in your position, I would give a sentence . . . that would incarcerate him for the rest of his natural life."

It was perhaps the only time a defense attorney has ever requested the maximum sentence for his client. Shortly before seven o'clock on the evening of January 18, 1967, Albert Henry DeSalvo was led away in handcuffs to begin concurrent ten-year sentences and a consecutive life sentence. Under Massachusetts law, the earliest he could be released was 1993. The question of whether or not he had killed thirteen women in the Boston area had still not been answered. And the question of whether or not he had killed one woman on Scott Road had hardly even been asked.

TWENTY-FOUR

ROY SMITH WAS thirty-five or thirty-six years old and facing natural life without hope of parole. Hopelessness, the Department of Corrections is well aware, breeds desperation, so incentives are built into the system to encourage even men with nothing to lose to obey the rules. If you obey the rules, you get privileges. If you break the rules, you lose them. If you break enough rules, you wind up in solitary confinement with only an hour of exercise a day. Man is a social animal, and the threat of solitary is usually enough to keep all but the most troubled inmates in line.

When Roy Smith was convicted, all adult men in Massachusetts were sentenced to what was then called MCI-Walpole or MCI-Concord and then dispersed throughout the prison system. Walpole had a murder a month and was one of the most violent prisons in the country. A weapons sweep in the 1970s turned up three guns hidden inside the walls at Walpole. Enough money would get you anything you needed in Walpole, including murder. There were prison riots at Walpole and inmate killings and inmate rapes and a poisonous racial atmosphere that essentially divided the prison into two violent camps.

Despite the brutality of the crime of which he'd been convicted, Smith was not a man inclined toward mayhem—he was barely even inclined toward talking to other people—and it must have been immediately apparent to prison officials that he did not belong at Walpole. Within weeks of his incarceration Smith was transferred to MCI-Norfolk, which, by contrast, was one of the most progressive prisons in the country. Inmates at Norfolk lived in unlocked rooms and moved freely around in the dormitory halls. They were allowed to cook for themselves and they were allowed to buy food at the commissary store with money they earned at various prison jobs and they were allowed to keep vegetable gardens and the very best of them were allowed to work outside the prison. The punishment for persistent bad behavior at Norfolk was leaving Norfolk. That was a fate most inmates tried to avoid.

It was two days after Christmas when Smith made the trip from Walpole to Norfolk in the back of a prison van. A light snow was falling that would turn into a brief intense snow squall after dark. If he'd cared to, Smith could have looked out through the steel mesh that covered the windows and watched the dark pine forests of southeastern Massachusetts roll by. Dusted with snow against an iron sky, the forests would not have looked like a place Smith might escape into and hide; they would have looked like a place where he would die. Fields slid by, left over from when Massachusetts was mostly farmland, and then tidy little houses with shingled roofs and painted fences. Norfolk appears suddenly out of the woods, a nineteen-foot gray cement wall wrapped around a cluster of brick dormitories built by inmates the year Roy Smith was born. Smith would have seen the black slate roofs of the dormitories beyond the wall and then the gray stone-block administration building that fronted the road. Across the road was an old farmhouse bracketed by huge chestnut trees; that was where the warden lived. Beyond the warden's house was a road that ran behind the prison and then the forest again, silenced now by falling snow. The van stopped in front of the administration building and the driver got out and unlocked the back, and Smith stepped out awkwardly in his leg-irons and chains. He climbed the granite steps to the entrance one at a time and paused while the guard got the door for him. Then he stepped once and for all into prison and out of the world.

The receiving room had a handsome slate floor and a high ceiling and a control center made of bolted steel plate that was painted battleship gray. Smith shuffled forward into the pedestrian trap and the first door closed behind him and then the second door opened and he stepped outside the trap and the second one closed behind him and the guard led him upstairs to a jail cell to be processed. Smith had his shackles unlocked and he was weighed and measured and given a medical checkup to make sure he wasn't bringing diseases like tuberculosis into the prison. Then he was handed his prison clothes: a pair of dungaree pants, a white T-shirt, a dungaree shirt, a black sweatshirt, visiting-day clothes, and a blue wool Eisenhower jacket. All his clothes would eventually have his name on the back, as if he were a basketball star.

Norfolk was designed in the 1920s by a penologist named Howard Gill, who had a reputation of being idealistic almost to the point of craziness. He is now thought simply to have been way ahead of his time. Gill designed Norfolk to look like a college campus—he possibly had Yale in mind—with a dozen or so brick dormitories and administrative buildings arranged around a huge grass quad. Inmates could only walk counterclockwise around the quad. Walking around the quad for the first time, Smith would have looked up to see the tops of the white pines that came almost to the edge of the prison walls. Inside those walls was a dead zone of mowed grass and then an electric fence topped with barbed wire. Norfolk is a medium-security prison with maximum-security walls. No one has ever escaped over the walls, though inmates have occasionally made it out through the vehicle trap, hidden in a barrel or a bag of trash.

Hanging from two I beams at the far end of the quad was a steel train wheel with a small section hacksawed out to produce a better tone. When the wheel was hit with a sledgehammer, it rang with a sound that could be heard everywhere in the prison, and that was how inmates knew it was time to return to their dorms. The first ring meant, Start moving, and the second ring came five minutes later and meant, You'd better already be where you were going. Meals were prepared in an enormous basement kitchen and wheeled on carts through a system of tunnels to the inmate dorms. The tunnels linked every building in the prison with every other building and allowed prisoners to eat in their own dining room rather than in a prison cafeteria with men they didn't know. The tunnels and group meals were an essential part of Gill's vision of community-based prison life.

Evaluations of Smith written years later noted that he was "slowly coming out of his shell." According to other inmates, however, he had almost no friends at all. At Walpole he had worked in the machine shop, and at Norfolk he did a year in the clothing shop before requesting kitchen duty. He soon found himself cooking for almost eight hundred men. Meal preparation was the least-favorite job in the prison because the kitchen was hot as a sauna and the work was so hard, but Smith may have found some solace in it. Each meal was a massive undertaking under tremendous time pressure, and maybe that was something he could lose himself in. Much of the food was cooked in eighty-gallon steel-jacketed cauldrons that were stirred with wooden blades big enough to paddle canoes. It was brutal work that, if nothing else, might have put some muscle on the skinny Smith.

He must have done well in the general kitchen because after some years he was promoted to the smaller gatehouse kitchen, outside the prison walls. He worked there without supervision—he could have walked away anytime he wanted—and was eventually put in charge of a six-man staff. There was an inmate council at Norfolk made up of elected representatives from each dorm, but Smith saw no reason to involve himself in that. Nor did he play football or basketball or softball or join the debate team. In the 1970s the Harvard debate team took on the Norfolk debate team in the prison auditorium and lost. Semiprofessional sports teams also came to Norfolk to play the inmates and—for the most part—to lose. Smith was a heavy smoker and showed every sign of being deeply depressed, both of which would have kept him off the field, but he certainly would have watched the games. They were exciting, savage events—the football in particular—and even the prison staff found themselves cheering from the sidelines.

ONE OF THE truisms about prison is that every prisoner claims he is innocent; the other is that only the prisoners know which ones really are. The truly innocent are both a kind of prison royalty and uniquely damned, and for one reason or another, Roy Smith joined their ranks. It may have been because word got out that he had refused a plea bargain before his trial. The Middlesex

DA's office had offered Smith a deal in which he would plead guilty to second-degree murder in exchange for a fifteen-year sentence. For a first-time murderer facing the death penalty it would have been a deal worth considering. He didn't. Smith's reputation as innocent could only have been reinforced by his first clemency hearing. Because parole boards generally insist that an inmate express regret for his crime, the hearings present an excruciating choice for the truly innocent. Do you salvage something of your life by mouthing regret for a crime you didn't commit, or do you insist on your innocence and stay in prison until you die? For what it's worth, Smith again refused to admit having anything to do with Bessie Goldberg's murder.

"Roy was extremely polite," says George Bohlinger, superintendent at Norfolk while Smith was there. "He was not an ass kisser under any circumstances, he was just a gentleman. And you knew it right away. There's probably not a person in that institution that doesn't say, 'I'm innocent,' or, 'I committed four murders but I'm in here for one I didn't do.' But I remember Roy telling me he didn't do it, and he was one of the few people—and there *were* some—where you had to think, 'He didn't do it.'"

When George Bohlinger took over Norfolk in the early 1970s, he was thirty-two years old and the youngest state prison warden in the country. His philosophy about discipline was that he could bring an inmate to his knees faster with a pencil than with a billy club. Bohlinger lived for a while in a room in one of the inmate dorms and walked freely around the quad and would stand and talk to groups of inmates as long as he could keep his back to something. He still cannot be in a group of people without having his back to the wall. At any given time there were a hundred or so unarmed officers at Norfolk supervising about eight hundred inmates. A hundred men cannot get eight hundred men to do *anything* without their consent, and in a prison as wide open as Norfolk, that required a delicate balance of power.

"You run the prison with the cooperation of the inmates," says Bohlinger. "The way Norfolk was set up, it was the hardest prison to control inside the walls that I knew of in the country. We were the first operation in the country or the world to follow the UN guidelines for prison reform. We signed it inside the yard at Norfolk."

For the most part Gill's vision worked, though Bohlinger had constantly to be on guard against scams. Swallowing razor blades wrapped in tin foil was briefly in vogue among inmates, for example, because the razor blades easily showed up on an X-ray and required a trip to Shattuck hospital. On the fifty-minute drive the lucky inmate could feast his eyes on everything—cars, houses, trees, and of course women—that was missing from his life. This was not just an amusing little gambit; one inmate went on to escape from Shattuck by carving a pistol from a bar of soap and coloring it black with shoe polish.

Unlike his life on the outside, Smith left little record of his time at Norfolk because he almost never got into trouble. In 1967 he got into a fight with another inmate over a chair, and in 1971 he was caught smuggling yeast out of the kitchen to use in making home brew, but that was it. (The inmates fermented cafeteria ketchup into a primitive moonshine known as Big Red that tasted like hell but produced the desired effect. Corrections officers could smell it fermenting up in the attics and were constantly rooting around up there trying to find it.) Smith's behavior was so good that his record was described as "nearly flawless" at later clemency hearings. In addition to working in the kitchen, he eventually completed college-level courses in abnormal psychology, biology, cultural anthropology, and Western civilization. He also helped other inmates study for the high school equivalency diploma. For a black man from Mississippi who quit school in eighth grade, it was an impressive accomplishment. It is possible that at some point during his long incarceration, Roy Smith had the strange thought that he'd made more of himself in prison than he ever had on the outside. This was exactly what Howard Gill had envisioned when he built Norfolk; this was exactly what the Massachusetts Department of Corrections meant when they stated in a report: "If a man is returned to society more embittered, vengeful, demoralized and incapable of social and economic survival than when he first came to prison, then we certainly . . . have failed to protect society."

Still, Smith's life was going by, and at times the thought of it left him shaking with rage. While in prison he learned that one of his brothers had died, that Carol Bell had taken his son to live in New Jersey, and finally that she had died as well. Scooter moved in with Carol's parents and eventually stopped communicating with Smith altogether. He was helpless to do anything about any of it. Occasionally he called home to Oxford and talked with his parents, and occasionally he sent them money from his prison jobs. He also tried to maintain a relationship with his sister's son, Coach— named after one of Roy's brothers—but it was almost impossible on the phone. Roy Smith, who had drifted through his life avoiding, or destroying, any kind of domestic attachments, was now in the odd position of trying to reach out to people, and failing.

Several years into his term he started exchanging letters with a woman named Nanette Emmanuel, who wrote him after reading about his case in the *Boston Globe*. Smith's first letters to her talked about prison life and his efforts to get a new trial, but as the years went by, they got angrier and angrier until they were almost unreadable. He wound up accusing virtually everyone trying to help him on the outside of not doing enough and, ultimately, of sabotaging him. "I ain't seen or heard from Cohen since December 25, 1967," Smith wrote about his lawyer in the fall of 1968. "I don't know if he's working on my case or not, I can't understand it but I do know it's driving me crazy. Four years waiting on that man, I just get so mad I could scream." One month later he wrote: "Cohen lie for the fun of it, I don't trust him, I just can't let that man fool me again for a year I couldn't stand it. I'm too depressed. And you were right, Nixon did win and he's another Wallace just as low and dirty. Nixon never did anything for no one, this world are truly a mess."

Smith's case had, in fact, become a small sensation. Beryl Cohen—who undoubtedly avoided contact with the enraged Smith because he had no good news to tell him—teamed up with another Boston lawyer named Neil Chayet to work on his case. They coordinated their efforts with a Cambridge city councilwoman named Barbara Ackerman, who had helped establish something called the Roy Smith Defense Fund. The defense fund hired Steve Delaney— the same Delaney who had come to my parents' house to talk to my mother—to reinvestigate the crime. Delaney sought the help of a *Boston Globe* reporter named Ray Richards, who had tried to confirm rumors that the Middlesex DA's office had threatened two female witnesses with cutting off their benefits under Aid to Dependent Children if they didn't testify. After more than a year of chasing these rumors, Barbara Ackerman sent Smith a typed letter saying that she couldn't do anything to help him unless he persuaded the two women, who were friends of his, to sign an affidavit stating that they had been coerced. Otherwise his best chance was a governor's pardon based on good behavior.

As well-intentioned people on the outside did their best and gradually lost interest, Smith railed on. He fired Cohen and then rehired him a year later. He told off Ray Richards to his face during a prison visit. He fired off bombshell letters to Ackerman, to Chayet, to Delaney, to everyone but Emmanuel herself. Interspersed in the vitriol of his letters were inquiries about Emmanuel's love life and comments on world events. Through the bars of his cell, as it were, Smith watched America go through some of the most violent upheavals of its history. In 1967 he watched the Supreme Court finally strike down laws in sixteen states holding that interracial marriage was illegal. He watched the U.S. military get dragged into a war in Vietnam, and he watched a black activist named Stokely Carmichael refuse military service by declaring famously, "Ain't no Vietcong ever called me nigger. If I'm gonna do any fighting, it's going to be right here at home." (A variation of this quote was later used by boxing legend Muhammad Ali, to whom it is often attributed.) He watched National Guard units suppress a race riot in Detroit by raking the ghetto rooftops with bursts from .50-caliber machine guns. The guns were mounted in turrets atop armored personnel carriers and were identical to the weapons that were clearing jungle around Khe Sanh. Smith watched Martin Luther King get shot down on a motel balcony and Robert Kennedy get shot down outside a Los Angeles ballroom and an openly racist presidential candidate named George Wallace get shot down, but not killed, in Laurel, Maryland. He watched poorly trained National Guardsmen open fire at Kent State University and kill four white students who were protesting the U.S. invasion of Cambodia. He watched inmates at Attica Correctional Facility in upstate New York take dozens of corrections officers hostage in an attempt to improve their living conditions. State troopers started shooting indiscriminately into the prison yard and killed forty-three people, including ten of the officers they were trying to save. Afterward the surviving inmates were forced to strip naked and run over broken glass while troopers beat them with clubs.

Of all the violence going on outside the walls of Norfolk, it was the murder of Martin Luther King that hit Smith the hardest. King was killed by a single round from a 30.06 rifle that struck him in the neck while he was leaning over a balcony railing, talking to a musician named Ben Branch. The death came at a time when Roy Smith was particularly dispirited about his case and, in some ways, about the state of his country. "Nothing new about me and nothing in sight and nothing have come down about me," he wrote in a letter one week after the murder. "I think this is only another month gone by. And on top of that the brutal slaying of Dr. Martin Luther King. This nation is sick and have a lot to answer for, but I know it's good peoples in this world and I hope what he lived and died for will open everyone's heart. Or we will all perish together, and until the black man get justice, it will always be hell on earth."

For a black man in prison around 1968, America must indeed have looked like hell on earth. Attica aside, it must have looked like a country where it was almost safer to be inside a prison—where the cops had no guns—than out.

TWENTY-FIVE

ALBERT DESALVO, Bridgewater Correctional Institution: "I am not in control of myself. I know that something awful has been done, that the whole world of human beings are shocked and will be even more shocked, that people everywhere are saying, My God, is this a man? But it can't be helped, I am what I am. I go looking around the apartment. I put out drawers, I go into the bathroom again and I throw things down on the floor, towels, I pull out the drawer in the pantry, I go into the living room and I find her pocketbook, I dump it out on the divan, I don't think I took a thing. . . . I don't know what I want.

"Now I go back to her. She is sitting there on the bed. I put the stocking around her throat and knot it twice, good and tight, then I put a loose pink and white thing around and tie it into a big bow. It's hard to talk about what I did then. I think, looking back on it, that it had something to do with a killing that was a mark, something like the end of something, you understand me? I went into the kitchen. I don't know why I did this. I get a broom and I go back into the bedroom. Well, she was on the bed and she had these things around her neck and this stocking and this scarf and the other thing. I was just a different person altogether, these things were going on and the feeling after I got out of the apartment was that it never happened. But now I stood there with the broom and looking at her I begin to get angry, she make me angry, just to look at her, I don't know why.

"I go over to the bed and I take the broom handle and put it into her, I push it into her but not so far as to hurt her. You say it is funny that I worry about hurting her when she is already dead, but that is the truth . . . I don't want to hurt her. I leave it there and she look like a woman with things being done to her. I stand there and look, then go around the apartment again. I find this card, it says, 'Happy New Year.' I go back to her and put it at her right foot, I lean it against her foot.

"When I go out of there it was like it never happened. I mean, it is just as if I was coming out of something, you understand me? I go out and I got downstairs and, as far as I was concerned, it wasn't me. I can't explain it to you any other way. It's just so unreal. I was there. It was done. I don't deny it. And yet if you talked to me an hour later, it didn't mean nothing. Now I go down and out of that place and when I get to Charles Street it is dark. I even stand for a minute in the doorway and already the whole thing is fading out in my mind, but I want to tell you, too, that something important has happened to me here. I don't know what—that is not for guys like me to figure, which is why I have been saying that I need help for so long. But I feel it. And just for a minute I stand there, then I go along into the darkness of the Back Bay. And it seems to me that no more women will ever see the Boston Strangler again."

TWENTY-SIX

AT 10:00 A.M. ON February 24, 1967, the FBI office in Boston issued an urgent teletype that three inmates had escaped from Bridgewater prison, a facility that served as a mental hospital for criminals. All three men worked in the kitchen and were supposed to wake up half an hour before the rest of the inmates to help prepare breakfast, but when a guard stopped at their adjoining cells at 6:20 that morning, they were gone. One of the men had gotten hold of a skeleton key and had reached through a slot in his solid wooden door and opened it from the outside. The locks were massive brass mechanisms installed in 1888, but the company that built them had gone out of business, so the prison staff had to keep them in repair with improvised parts. They were not hard locks to breach.

The three men proceeded down their cell block corridor, unlocking any doors that blocked their passage, and then climbed into an elevator shaft that had been knocked open for repairs. From the elevator shaft they were able to make it outside the building and onto the top of a twenty-foot-high brick wall. They walked northward along the top of the wall until it hit the outer walls of the prison, and then they jumped down to the ground. Police found three sets of footprints in the snow that led across the old farm fields surrounding the prison and then hopped across a small creek. From there they disappeared into the dense pine woods that lay beyond the fields. One of the escapees was a forty-year-old man named Frederick Erickson who was serving a life sentence for killing his wife. The second was an armed robber named George Harrison who had a reputation for being trigger-happy. The third was Albert DeSalvo.

Erickson and Harrison wound up at a cocktail lounge in Waltham later that day, where they called a lawyer and waited for the police to pick them up. They said that after escaping from the prison in the middle of the night they had walked to Bridgewater State College, stolen a car, and dropped DeSalvo off in Boston before driving north. They ran out of gas in the town of Everett, abandoned the car, and made their way back toward Boston. DeSalvo seemed to show a little more determination: "De Salvo indicated intention of going to Ontario, Canada by plane to get a 'nose job,'" an FBI teletype warned the following day, undoubtedly based on information provided by Erickson and Harrison. "After which he would kill the doctor performing the operation. De Salvo alleged to be armed with an eight shot thirty-two caliber Beretta. De Salvo carries gun in rectum and plans to use if necessary."

Why DeSalvo would carry the Beretta in his rectum—or how he planned to extract it in an emergency—was not explained. The information was obviously made up, but the FBI alerted both Canada and Mexico, and then started searching for DeSalvo in the small town of Lynn, north of Boston. The focus on Lynn was based on a tip that Erickson and Harrison had actually dropped DeSalvo off there rather than in Boston. The police also arrested DeSalvo's two brothers and accused them of complicity in the escape, though that may just have been a way of putting pressure on him. At two o'clock the following afternoon, Lynn police got a call from the owner of Simmons Uniform Store, who said that DeSalvo was in his store and wanted to give himself up. He'd walked in wearing an ill-fitting sailor's uniform that he'd stolen from a private home the previous night, and he had asked to use the store phone to call his lawyer. The store owner asked if he was Albert DeSalvo, DeSalvo said that he was, and the owner frisked him and then led him into the back of the store. He let DeSalvo use the phone while he made him a cup of coffee, and DeSalvo had just taken his first sip when the police came in and put the cuffs on.

Word got out almost immediately that DeSalvo had been caught, and a crowd of two thousand people massed around the Lynn police station to see him. They were held in check by state troopers with shotguns. "Maybe people will know what it means to be mentally ill," DeSalvo told the crowd as he was led inside. At an impromptu press conference he went on to tell reporters that he had escaped only to draw attention to the fact that he wasn't getting the psychological help he'd been promised. "I didn't mean no harm to nobody," he said. "I did it to bring it back to the attention of the public that a man has a mental illness and hires a lawyer, and no one does anything about it."

The reason he was not getting psychological help was because Bridgewater was closer to a nineteenth-century lunatic asylum than to a mental hospital. On most days there was only one doctor on duty to care for more than six hundred inmates. Until recently seventy-five inmates had been jammed into an old boiler room with a dirt floor that turned white with frost in the winter. A third of the inmates had completed their criminal sentences but were still behind bars because the state didn't know what to do with them. One of these unfortunates had been picked up for vagrancy in 1905 and was still trying to get out. Conditions were so unspeakable that men charged with crimes were pleading guilty and doing their time at Walpole rather than risking a psychological evaluation at Bridgewater.

DeSalvo's escape got him seven more years and a transfer to Walpole. Bridgewater was the only prison in the state that could make Walpole feel like a relief. The word on the cell blocks, though, was that DeSalvo was going to be killed as soon as he got there, so he was put in the hospital ward under twenty-four-hour guard. Eventually he was transferred to maximum security and finally to the general inmate population. It was a dramatic start to his life sentence, but DeSalvo was both tough and likable, and it did not take long for him to carve out a place for himself in the violent, racially charged world of Walpole prison.

"Organized crime, they were their own group," says a former state trooper named Ted Harvey about the power structure at Walpole. Harvey had been part of the trooper detail that had broken up the riots that swept through Walpole in the early seventies. "And in those days the Muslims were in big, big time; they stayed right with themselves. There was an Irish mafia that stayed by themselves, and the Italian mafia, and if you killed a little boy or a little girl, you'd have to be in protective custody because they'd kill you. Let's say I wasn't a state trooper, let's just say I was Teddy Harvey from Salem and got involved in some shit, well, they size you up in about thirty seconds. You get a Dorchester kid or a Charlestown kid, you ain't gonna bother him, you'll leave him alone 'cause he'll kill you. He'll take his beating and then he'll just get you, that's all. You get guys like you or me that never did anything wrong in their lives, we end up in prison, we ain't gonna make it."

They get turned into punks, Harvey said, which was prison slang for sexual slaves. They became more and more effeminate and sub-servient until they were completely destroyed psychologically.

According to Harvey, DeSalvo got by in prison because he even-tually secured a job in the prison dispensary where he was able to steal—or buy from the guards—pharmaceuticals that went for a high price on the cell blocks. With that money he made friends or bought himself protection or just turned himself into someone whom no one wanted as an enemy. He also made necklaces and sold them at the prison gift shop under the name, "Chokers by DeSalvo." They sold for as much as ten dollars each and were so in demand that DeSalvo was clearing up to three thousand dollars a year. A photograph taken at Walpole after the riots shows DeSalvo—palms up, mouth open in midsentence—talking to reporters in front of a group of much younger inmates. He's been there eight years at this point, and his broad shoulders have shrunk a bit, his handsome face has gotten puffier, sadder, a little ruined around the eyes. But he's the one talking. The other men stand patiently around him with their arms folded across their chests because—or so it appears—they are content to let DeSalvo do their speaking for them.

It was around this same time that DeSalvo received a request for an interview from Steve Delaney, the private detective who had talked to my mother about his work at out house. Delaney was now drawing a paycheck from the Roy Smith Defense Fund and trying to uncover evidence that Smith was innocent. That inevitably meant pursuing the idea that DeSalvo could have committed the Goldberg murder. In November 1970 Delaney showed up at

Walpole and met with DeSalvo in a small visiting room. The guard who let Delaney in told him that the door would be locked behind him and added sarcastically, Enjoy your interview.

DeSalvo knew why Delaney was there because Delaney was required to declare his intentions in a letter before the visit. You're wasting your time, I didn't do the Bessie Goldberg murder, DeSalvo told Delaney as soon as he stepped into the room. Delaney had just gotten his private investigator's license a year earlier, but he was a skillful interviewer with a phenomenal mind for details, and he was not thrown by DeSalvo's declaration. He sat down and started asking him about the other Boston Stranglings. It was a chess game that—perhaps out of sheer boredom—DeSalvo was willing to play. Delaney knew that killers who are reluctant to talk about their own crimes will sometimes talk about them in hypothetical terms, and that was the approach he tried. He picked his way carefully around the topic with questions like, If a guy were going to kill that many women, how would he do it? How would he break into their apartments? How would he attack them without getting hurt?

Whether DeSalvo was truly the Strangler or not, the questions were too much for him to resist. During his time in prison he had gone from insisting that he was the Boston Strangler to insisting— after his escape—that he wasn't. His confessions had gained him nothing, and there was no reason to continue claiming that he had killed thirteen women. He had told Delaney point-blank that he was not the Boston Strangler, but he went on to turn the tables. If I *were* the Strangler, he said, how do *you* think I would do it? Delaney suggested some possibilities for killing women in their apartments and went on to ruminate on what might be the best way to attack someone, once you had them alone in a room. You would want it to be quick. You wouldn't want to get hurt—even scratched—because that would be evidence against you. You would want to go from being a normal person to a killer and then back in at most a few minutes. It's not an easy thing to do.

While Delaney was suggesting various scenarios, DeSalvo got up from his seat and said, Stand up, this will only take a minute. Delaney stood up and glanced out the window to see if he could see the guard. There was no one in sight. The next thing he knew, DeSalvo's arm was around his neck. "He put his bicep and his forearm on each side and flexed," Delaney says. "He said, 'See how I'm not hurting any of the bones but I'm cutting off your air?' And slowly but surely I could see: You know how they pump up your arm for blood pressure? It was the same kind of feeling but increasing; I think it was just the blood building up, you know? And I started feeling pain, and I was like, okay, I get the point. He said, 'Go ahead, do something. Do anything you want. Kick me. Punch me.' I couldn't, I knew I couldn't, I wasn't about to stomp or kick him, I just wanted him to let me go."

DeSalvo had clearly discovered the carotid takedown, and now Delaney was strangling to death in the most secure prison in the state. The guard on the other side of the wall either didn't know or didn't care. DeSalvo finally let Delaney go and then went straight back into his denial that he was the Boston Strangler. He went on to tell Delaney that he knew for a fact that Roy Smith had flunked a lie detector test. He even boasted that he knew which questions Smith had missed.

Smith had begged to take a lie detector test in the Belmont police station, but the police had refused. Eight years into his sentence— just a couple of months before Delaney's visit to Walpole—he finally arranged for one at Norfolk, but according to Delaney, the results were unusable. When people take lie detector tests, they also answer a series of mildly provocative questions—Have you ever lied to a friend? Are you ashamed of anything you have done?—to establish a baseline response that the crime-related questions can be measured against. If a subject's blood pressure rises to a certain level when answering a question about lying to a friend—something virtually everyone has done—it shouldn't rise much beyond that when saying that he didn't kill Bessie Goldberg. If he's lying because he did, in fact, kill Bessie Goldberg, his blood pressure will skyrocket. It is a physiological response that almost no one can control.

The problem comes when a suspect is so upset about the circumstances he is in that that every question, no matter how neutral, is wildly disturbing. He becomes an "untestable subject," and according to Delaney, that was what happened to Smith. When the tester gave Smith the control questions, his physiological responses were so extreme that no baseline could be established. The technician who administered the test had a much more skeptical interpretation of Smith's reactions, however. He reported that the test results "did not support his account of his activities, especially relating to . . . the death of Bessie Goldberg." That still did not necessarily mean that Smith had killed Bessie Goldberg; it just meant that the test would not help him get out of Norfolk. Lie detector tests are good investigative tools, but test results are not admissible in court because their error rates are on the order of 30 percent. There was still a one-in-three chance that Smith was telling the truth.

But it was interesting that DeSalvo knew about Smith in the first place. When he first confessed to thirteen murders, he denied having anything to do with Bessie Goldberg. He did, however, describe the incident in our studio when he was on the ladder and my mother came in back to tell him about the murder. He told investigators that he was so shocked he almost fell off the ladder. He also described the

Goldberg house to John Bottomly, though he said that he knew what it looked like because he had seen a photograph in the newspaper. "It was, like, a two—a single family home, the shades were all down, white shades," DeSalvo told Bottomly. "It was brick, a red brick house and it had the drainpipes on the right, square type."

Boston had a murder a week in those days, and of all those murders, DeSalvo had chosen to memorize the newspaper photos of *that* one. Whether or not DeSalvo had ever been at the Goldberg house, the newspaper photo was clearly the source of his description. All the shades were pulled down because police investigators were in the house, and that was when the photograph had been taken. And DeSalvo's description was supremely detailed: Israel Goldberg himself probably didn't even know whether he had round gutters or square, yet DeSalvo did—and he did despite the fact that it was almost impossible to tell which kind they were from the photograph. DeSalvo would have had to study it very, very hard.

His fascination made sense, though, no matter what his relationship with the Goldberg murder might be. If DeSalvo had killed thirteen women but *not* Bessie Goldberg, his fascination would lie in the fact that another man had committed a copycat crime a mile away from where he was working. If DeSalvo had killed all the women, *including* Bessie Goldberg, his fascination would lie in the fact that an innocent man was doing time for a crime that he, DeSalvo, had committed. (If he was sufficiently racist or hardhearted, he might even find the situation entertaining.) The scenario in which he would be the least fascinated would be the one in which he hadn't actually killed anyone but claimed that he had. In that case a solved murder that was not considered part of the Strangler series would be of absolutely no interest—or use—to him at all. It would be a waste of time, a dud.

Even to begin evaluating whether DeSalvo is the Boston Strangler, one has to decide whether one man could be capable of all the murders he claimed. If not, the very term "Boston Strangler" is a false proposition. Some psychologists at the time felt that the diversity of victims—young and old, black and white, strangled and not strangled, raped and not raped—meant that several murderers were at work. That conclusion fits the classic model for serial killers, who tend to not vary their routine, but doesn't encompass all of them. In the 1920s, a former mental patient named Earle Leonard Nelson went on an eighteen-month rampage around the United States and Canada that left over twenty women dead. Nelson initially preyed on elderly women who ran boarding houses—just the sort places where he could easily pass unnoticed—but then he started killing young women. All his victims were first strangled and then raped, and some were found with a belt or dishrag wound tightly around their neck. Nelson was dubbed the "Dark Strangler" because of his swarthy complexion. He was finally caught in Manitoba, Canada, and hanged on January 13, 1928.

So the age range of the Boston victims does not necessarily mean that there were multiple killers; they could all have been killed by one man who switched propensities the way Nelson did. The next question is timing. The psychological mechanism that compels a person to commit a sex murder is not in a constant state of readiness; it waxes and wanes like every other form of mental illness. When a sex murderer loses control of himself, murdering one person does not necessarily stabilize him again; if anything it may open the door to other—sometimes worse—possibilities. If, for argument's sake, you include Bessie Goldberg in the list of Strangler victims, a pattern starts to emerge. Of the fourteen murders attributed to the "Boston Strangler," the first ten occurred in distinct groupings. Slesers, Mullen, Nichols, and Blake were killed within a two-week period at the end of June 1962. (Mary Mullen was the woman who DeSalvo claimed had died of a heart attack when he started to strangle her.) Irga and Sullivan were killed within hours of each other in early September 1962, Clark and Bissette were killed within three weeks of each other in December 1962, and Brown and Goldberg were killed within days of each other in March 1963. The next four murders occurred individually and months apart, until they stopped altogether with the killing of Mary Sullivan, on January 4, 1964.

If this was the work of several men, it is almost certain that some of them would have been caught. In those years the Boston Homicide Division was solving roughly half of all murders, and there was no reason for the Strangler murders to be any different. One could make sense of this pattern, though, by seeing it as the work of one man. Whoever he might be, his initial loss of control was the worst and most savage, resulting in four murders in two weeks. Subsequent binges of violence were limited to pairs of people and then, finally, to one person at a time. The killer looked very much like a man who was wrestling with the demons inside him and needed a year and a half finally to get the upper hand. After that he may have lived in terror that "the feeling" would overwhelm him again and he would return to killing. The fact that he had deliberately murdered people did not necessarily mean that he wanted to be doing that; like an abusive husband, he may have been secretly horrified by his crimes. Such a man might well ask for help before it happened again. Such a man might well beg to be stowed away in a secure place, like a hospital or a prison, until the problem was under control. Such a man, in fact, might well ask for life in prison—as DeSalvo did—rather than risk an outbreak like the one he had just been through.

DeSalvo—with his brutal childhood, sexual obsessions, and history of rapes and assaults—was an excellent candidate for such a person. The problem was that his confessions were both somewhat inaccurate and hopelessly polluted by prompting from John Bottomly, and there was no physical evidence, not one shred, that linked him to any of the crimes. And yet. How can one ignore a man whose confessions to thirteen murders are even *somewhat* accurate? How can one ignore a man who asks to be incarcerated for life so that his psychological problems can be studied? The authorities, at least, could not. On September 17, 1965, days after DeSalvo had given his last confession to Bottomly, J. Edgar Hoover received a cable about DeSalvo from the Boston bureau of the FBI. The cable left the alleged confessions completely unaddressed, but said that the Massachusetts AG's office was "pretty much satisfied" they had identified the Boston Strangler. "He had picked out of a large number of photos the ten women he had strangled," the cable read, referring to DeSalvo. "This individual also advised that there was an eleventh person whom he had murdered, the picture of whom was not in the group."

This was no great feat; photographs of the victims had appeared in Boston area newspapers, and anyone with an even passing interest in the Strangler cases could have done the same thing. What was more impressive was that DeSalvo had known what was *not* in the pile. There was only one murder victim no one would recognize because her brother had refused to release her photograph to the newspapers. It was Mary Brown, who had been beaten, raped, and strangled in Lawrence, Massachusetts, several days before Bessie Goldberg was killed. The crime was so savage and bloody that the police did not classify it as a Boston Strangling, and they had to go searching their records when DeSalvo brought it up two years later. DeSalvo's unsolicited claim that Mary Brown's photograph was missing from the pile sent investigators back to her brother, who finally gave them a photograph. Investigators inserted it into the pile, and DeSalvo picked her out "without delay."

Other than DeSalvo's guilt, there is only one explanation for how he could have identified her photograph. It would require either staggering incompetence or intentional fraud on the part of John Bottomly of the attorney general's office, but it is possible in the sense that all things are. Dr. Ames Robey, who was the medical director at Bridgewater prison at the time, testified at DeSalvo's rape trial that he was not insane. Privately Robey was convinced not only that DeSalvo had not killed anyone, but that he hadn't raped anyone either. All DeSalvo's rapes, Dr. Robey believed, were actually seductions, and the supposed rape victims had simply regretted their decision afterward and called the police. Decades later this was Dr. Robey's explanation for DeSalvo's performance with the photographs:

"Bottomly got very involved in [the Strangler investigation], among other things showing pictures to Albert, much like a lineup, of pictures that had not ever been published of the victims. We heard about it later because Albert couldn't help boasting, you know. Let's say you lay out a bunch of pictures, okay? And ordinarily I would go down them, and you're watching the pictures. Bottomly's face would have lost him a fortune in poker. DeSalvo just watched Bottomly's eyes and would go back to the right picture. I thought this thing smelled, so I called up Ed Brooke, [who] got the Supreme Court to issue a gag order on everyone concerned until they could hold a hearing. And, ah, no one ever bothered to get back to me on any of this."

Dr. Robey was not at the photo lineup, so it's unclear what he was basing his theory on. His theory also does not explain how

Bottomly could have signaled with his eyes that a photo was *not* there. Nevertheless, doubts persisted about DeSalvo's guilt, and they only increased after the prison break. Distraught that he had not been sent to a secure hospital to be studied as a serial killer, and unable to obtain a lucrative book deal about his life story, DeSalvo started denying that he was the Boston Strangler. True or not, the claims weren't gaining him anything, and there was no reason for him to continue with them.

DeSalvo's retreat spawned a host of conflicts. He tried to sue F. Lee Bailey for five million dollars after Bailey referred to him as the Boston Strangler on national television. He wrote a furious letter to the attorney general's office after Donald Conn, the prosecutor who had put him in prison, tried to run for attorney general on a platform that included claiming credit for putting the Boston Strangler behind bars. It was an audacious move, considering the fact that Conn had blocked any mention of the Stranglings during DeSalvo's rape trial. DeSalvo also hired another attorney to try to extract from Bailey money that was due him from a movie deal based on the Strangler murders. During all these convulsions in DeSalvo's prison-bound life, George Nassar remained his close adviser and confidant. They were always together in prison, speaking in low tones in the corridors. Nassar helped DeSalvo with his legal problems. Nassar gave him advice about how to promote himself in the outside world. Nassar, in the eyes of some, virtually became his literary agent.

In late November 1973, DeSalvo said something vague to his brother Richard about working on a manuscript that would reveal the "truth" about his life. About a week before Thanksgiving, DeSalvo checked himself into the prison hospital, which was a secure ward, complaining of stomach pains. Something was going

on in the prison, though, and it was possible he had done that simply to stay out of harm's way. On the evening of November 25,
which was a Sunday, he called Richard and had a lighthearted conversation with him and then called Dr. Ames Robey—whom he had
never liked—and asked to meet him the following morning. He said
it was urgent. The date was two days after the ten-year anniversary
of Roy Smith's conviction. Sometime after ten o'clock that night, a
man passed through four locked doors, entered DeSalvo's ward,
stabbed him sixteen times in the chest, and then covered him with
a hospital blanket so that no one would see the blood. DeSalvo
wasn't discovered until the following morning.

Whoever killed him had to have had some help; no one can get
through four locked doors at Walpole without someone else knowing about it. The prison warden thought that the murder was
related to DeSalvo's drug dealing in prison. Others thought he was
killed to keep him from revealing that the "real" Boston Strangler
was actually George Nassar. The fact that he was stabbed sixteen
times—often a sign of rage—suggested that revenge could have
been the motive. When my mother heard the news, she assumed
DeSalvo was killed by a black inmate in retaliation for Roy Smith's
conviction ten years earlier. Three inmates at Walpole were tried,
acquitted, tried again, and acquitted again for DeSalvo's murder,
and the case was finally dropped.

Like much about DeSalvo's life, his death remained a mystery.
DNA evidence was not yet something that investigators could make
use of, and when DeSalvo died, he took his secrets with him.

TWENTY-SEVEN

R OY SMITH WAS in prison ten years, a quarter of his life, when something shifted. Lifers generally do their time quietly, and Smith was no exception, but he somehow managed to distinguish himself in a way that most lifers don't: People started seriously to consider the possibility that he was innocent.

It is a quirk of human nature and maybe the justice system that—at least in Massachusetts in the 1970s—lifers were thought to be the most promising candidates for commutation. Most crimes, like robbery, assault, and rape, are committed by habitual offenders who have serious difficulty functioning peacefully in society. If they are released, around 50 percent of them go right back to committing their crimes. Murderers are different. If you exclude professional hit men and the insane, most murderers are in prison for a onetime eruption of violence that they themselves are often shocked to have committed. Once released, they have a recidivism rate of 2 percent. In a strictly statistical sense, murderers are much better candidates for judicial mercy than men who have committed far lesser crimes.

During those years the Massachusetts prison system was severely overcrowded, and the Advisory Board of Pardons was actively trying to release more lifers and low-risk inmates back into society. The board was traditionally composed of five members who were drawn, for the most part, from people in law enforcement jobs. In 1972 Massachusetts governor Francis Sargent expanded the board to seven members and made sure that three of them were reform-minded people who came from the civilian population. One of his new appointees was a former public defender named Paul Chernoff; another was a black minister from Roxbury named Michael Haynes. The Attica massacre had happened the previous year, and a wave of prison reform was sweeping the country that the law-and-order types couldn't hope to block. The Advisory Board of Pardons went from commuting one or two life sentences a year to commuting as many as sixteen.

In the fall of 1972, after the reforms had kicked in, Roy Smith sent a letter to a friend of Nanette Emmanuel's named Mrs. Joan Stevens. Stevens was married to a science reporter for the *New York Times* who had also taken an interest in Smith's case. "I am sorry to say I am not doing no kind of way good," he wrote Mrs. Stevens on October 13. "I am half out of my mind. I got myself enough time in—ten years, almost, and very easy Cohen could put in for a commutation. This year's the best I ever seen for people with life sentences, they are getting out right and left. The parole board is new and they believe in giving a man a chance, this year's been like cake and honey for lifers. All I want to do is get out and get me a job and get married and settle down. This year sure was a good chance for my freedom. Oh well, I don't know any more, I should be crazy by now."

Several months after he wrote that letter, his lawyer filed a petition with the Advisory Board of Pardons requesting a commutation hearing, and a date was eventually set for the following November. Smith wrote a letter to Ed Brooke, the former attorney general of Massachusetts who was now a senator in Washington, and persuaded him to put in a call on his behalf. He talked to George Bohlinger about giving a recommendation. He convinced several prison guards to write letters of support. One member of the advisory board even promised him a job if he got out. "Every move I made turned to gold," he wrote proudly to Joan Stevens after listing his small triumphs. "I sure been thinking about all of you, you can bet on that. Your letter found me hacking and coughing and I couldn't talk for a few days. Smile. This cold or whatever I got is something else, I got it when I went on leave for four days. Oh, you don't know, I been in Boston, this is the second time."

Smith's record at Norfolk was so clean that he had been included in a furlough program that gave him fourteen days a year of unsupervised time on the outside. He used one furlough to see a woman in Boston whom he described as his "girlfriend," and another to visit his lawyer, Beryl Cohen, at his home on Christmas Day. His ability to stay out of trouble on furlough was essential to being considered for commutation, and Smith went into his hearing with a record that was beyond reproach. His hearing was held inside Norfolk prison walls at 11 a.m. on Friday, November 30. The ten-year anniversary of his guilty verdict had passed a few days earlier, and Albert DeSalvo had been found dead on his hospital bed the previous Monday. The first hearing, for a small-time gangster named Joe Femino, ran an hour and a half late, so Smith's hearing didn't start until 12:30 that afternoon. Nanette Emmanuel, who had made the trip from Virginia for the hearing, testified about how hard Smith had worked to improve himself in prison. A friend of hers named Bill Parker, who was blind, told the board that Smith's first letters had shown "a certain immaturity," but that in the last three years he had undergone a profound change for the better. Theodore Restaino, assistant superintendent at Norfolk, testified that Smith was "the kind of guy he admires" in the institution. Beryl Cohen stood up and read letters that the guards at Norfolk had written and then described how Smith was erroneously thought to have been the Boston Strangler when he was arrested.

After a letter of opposition from Middlesex DA John Droney was read into the record, Smith was asked to testify. He sat before the seven members of the advisory board and answered questions for two and a half hours. Smith told them about growing up in Oxford, Mississippi. He told them about his military service. He told them about his young son in New Jersey who had no mother and, for the past ten years, no father as well. He told them about his efforts to educate himself. At one point a board member asked Smith how he'd managed to take college-level courses despite an eighth-grade education.

I learned myself and my room is a young library, Smith answered proudly. I'm not dumb or stupid or smart, I'm just in between.

The only worrisome moment came when they asked Smith about his lie detector test, and he could give them no easy answer for why he had not passed it. The hearing ended at 3:40, and afterward Smith, Cohen, Emmanuel, and Parker walked into the quad in the early winter dusk. Smith was ecstatic. All he had to do, he wrote to Joan Stevens, was wait a few weeks to find out whether the board had ruled in his favor. If they did, their recommendation would be on the governor's desk in months.

As far as Smith was concerned, he was halfway home.

———

IN THEORY THE commutation process in Massachusetts for murderers has nothing to do with guilt or innocence. A trial jury's decision on a man's guilt is considered to be the most sacred and untouchable aspect of the law, and the advisory board does not want to turn every commutation hearing, in effect, into a second trial. Neither does the board decide whether he has been "punished" enough, or whether his crime was exceptionally heinous; they simply decide whether the prisoner in question can become a productive member of society.

That is the theory. In practice, doubts about a petitioner's guilt cannot help but creep into the proceedings. And there is a good reason for that: A truly innocent petitioner would obviously make an excellent member of society, and since that is the very issue that the board is trying to determine, there is every reason for them to consider the possibility. They cannot decide a man's guilt, but they can use their doubts about his guilt to decide his fitness for civilian life. On January 7, 1974, the board finally met to decide on Smith's commutation. Their decision was quickly relayed to Beryl Cohen, who must have called Smith as soon as he got word. The advisory board, Cohen told him, had unanimously voted to recommend him to Governor Sargent for commutation. If the governor signed the papers and the Executive Council approved (this body reviewed all clemency pardons), Smith would be eligible for release on March 11, 1975, twelve years after the effective date of his life sentence.

Governor Sargent was a liberal republican in a liberal state who—unlike governors in some other states—did not particularly care if a commutation caused him political harm. He also had an unswerving sense of right and wrong and was unafraid to take positions that many other politicians wouldn't touch. He spoke at the first Earth Day; he ordered state flags to half-mast after the killings at Kent State; he backed legislation that disputed the legality of the Vietnam War. Still, his principles were not enough to win him reelection, and before he could sign Smith's commutation, he was pushed aside by a fiscal reformer named Michael Dukakis, who had promised to solve the state's financial crisis without raising taxes. Dukakis did balance the state budget, but he did it by putting through one of the biggest tax increases in Massachusetts history. That did not give him much political leeway on other issues, and when he took over the governor's office, he sent back for review the dozen or so commutations that were waiting on the governor's desk. Roy Smith's commutation was one of them.

By this point Smith was running the gatehouse kitchen, which served 150 staff meals a day, and working most days in an experimental work-release program at Medfield State Hospital. He wrote Joan Stevens that he was basically sleeping at the prison at night and not much more. This was about as good as the prison experience gets for a lifer, but it was far short of what Smith wanted. He was desperate to find his son in New Jersey, who was fourteen by now and could barely remember him, and he was desperate to have a steady relationship and a regular job. These were all things that had been beyond his reach before he went to prison, but he was capable of them now, and only a signature on a piece of paper stood in his way. The thought of it drove him crazy.

The magic day, March 11, 1975, came and went and still Smith was in prison. Spring turned into summer and summer into fall, and his commutation just seemed to make endless rounds between the advisory board, the governor's office, and the Executive Council. As infuriating as the process was, Smith could at least be reassured that he had virtually done the impossible: It was unheard of for a lifer to be considered for commutation after only ten years, and the only explanation was that a lot of people had to have doubts about Smith's guilt. Pardons Board Paul Chernoff gently alluded to this in his first recommendation to the governor's office: "During the more than ten years of his incarceration, Roy Smith has maintained his innocence of the murder of Mrs. Goldberg," Chernoff wrote. "The trial took place during the period of time in which the activities of the so-called 'Boston Strangler' were most fearful. Much public commentary speculated that Smith was the Strangler. The jury reached a verdict of guilty after only two hours." A later brief to the governor added: "It is the belief of the Advisory Board that further incarceration may constitute unfairness because of possible equities [*sic*] involved. The members are satisfied that further incarceration would serve no useful purpose."

As much as the advisory board might balk at the idea, the fact that Smith's possible innocence had affected their decision inevitably meant that they had acted to some degree like a trial jury. And as such, they were in the same position that Smith's jury had been in 1963: They were trying to determine an objective truth with subjective tools, and they would never know for sure whether they were right. There was one important difference, however. The board's best guess was based on their experience with an unending parade of truly guilty people, whereas the jury's best guess was based on their experience with one person who was possibly guilty. And in the board's opinion, Smith just seemed different. He did not seem like all the other guilty people they knew.

The least disturbing explanation for why this might be is that Smith was such an ingratiating charmer, and so relentlessly self-serving, that he managed to mold himself into exactly the kind of person that a liberal parole board would respond to in the mid-

1970s. He conned them, in other words. The other possibility is a lot more troubling: that Smith was truly innocent. And if he was truly innocent, the Massachusetts judicial system—at least as it existed in 1963—failed not only Smith and the Goldberg family but also, in some sense, every other person in the state.

FOUR DECADES LATER the only way to know with absolute certainty whether Smith was guilty would be to compare DNA taken from the semen inside Bessie Goldberg with DNA taken from Smith's body. If they matched, he raped and killed her, end of story. But no state keeps evidence indefinitely, and the rape kit that was collected at the crime scene has long since been destroyed. Lacking DNA evidence, the only other way to improve upon the jury's wisdom of 1963 is take the evidence that existed at the time and retroactively apply forensic and legal advances that have occurred since then. If a forensic scientist were handed the crime report today, in other words, could he prove that Smith committed the rape? If a homicide prosecutor were handed the Bessie Goldberg murder file, would he be able to convict Smith? To indict him? To even arrest him?

The evidence of rape is the easiest to evaluate because it is a simple matter of physics and chemistry. In 2004 a forensic scientist named Karolyn Tontarski examined the autopsy reports from the Bessie Goldberg murder. (Tontarski used to work for the Massachusetts state police crime laboratory and is considered one of the top DNA experts in the country.) Her first conclusion was that the rape and murder had to have happened at the same time. If Bessie Goldberg had had sex with her husband a week earlier, as Israel Goldberg claimed, bacterial yeasts would have broken down virtually all the individual sperm cells in her vagina. In fact, there were "numerous intact spermatozoa" in a vaginal swab taken from her body, which meant that Bessie Goldberg almost certainly had sex the same day she was killed. If the sex had been consensual, gravity would have caused some of that semen to drain downward and stain her underwear after she stood up. There were no semen stains on her underwear, however, which meant that she never stood up after she was raped. She never stood up because she was dead.

The same basic principle applies to Roy Smith. If he raped Bessie Goldberg, semen and vaginal fluid would have stained his underwear when he pulled up his pants. But Smith was arrested in the same clothes that he'd been wearing the day of the murder, and there were no stains on his underwear and only a small one on the outside of his pants. "The sperm on Smith's zipper is not remarkable because of the absence of sperm on his underwear," says Tontarski. "The item of clothing closest to the body tends to have the most bodily fluid. The presence of sperm on a man's clothing, in and of itself, is not that remarkable—it was probably from a prior sexual encounter. There are inconsistencies with the analysis of Roy Smith's clothing which would indicate he was not the perpetrator."

Evaluating Smith's interrogation is more complicated because there is no way to prove by someone's behavior that he or she is lying. But you can come close. Interrogations are extremely stressful events, even for the innocent, and almost no one can completely control his or her responses when being questioned about a murder. A classic law enforcement manual called *Criminal Interrogation and Confessions* describes in detail the typical behaviors of an innocent and a guilty person. The guilty take, on average, three times longer to answer a direct question than the innocent. The guilty tend to touch their hair or their face or pick lint off their clothing when they talk. The guilty tend to repeat a question before they get around to answering it. The guilty tend to offer specific denials that are technically true—"I did not take $1,200 from the cash register yesterday!"—rather than general denials that are false. The guilty tend to apologize for the misunderstanding. The guilty tend to look for some sign of partial understanding. The guilty tend to use non-specific language about their actions that leaves wiggle room for later questions. The guilty tend to veer from angry to sullen to ingratiating and then back to angry again. The guilty tend to slouch in their chair, cross their arms, look away, and not move for long periods of time. The guilty, in other words, act guilty. Controlled studies have showed that trained investigators who watch *silent* videotapes of interrogations can correctly tell if a subject is lying 72 percent of the time. When the sound is turned on, their accuracy rises to 86 percent.

Innocent suspects are an entirely different matter. The innocent tend to get angry and stay angry. They tend to insist on continuing the interrogation until they are cleared as a suspect. They tend to sit straight up, look the questioner in the eye, and answer questions quickly if not eagerly. They tend to describe their actions in excruciating detail. They tend to continue voicing their denials even after they have been told to be quiet. The innocent, in short, see the interrogation not as an ordeal to be survived, but as an opportunity to clear their name. First and foremost the innocent tend to answer questions without having a lawyer by their side.

In 2004 a Boston homicide prosecutor named David Meier read a transcript of the interrogation of Roy Smith. (Meier had been chief prosecutor for the Suffolk County DA's office for the past ten years.) He also read the autopsy report on Bessie Goldberg and the state police crime report. Meier is an exceptional prosecutor in that he has not only put many murderers in prison but has also reversed previous murder convictions that were false. David Meier was asked to evaluate the Roy Smith case file—crime report, autopsy and interrogation—as if it had landed on his desk today.

The first thing that strikes Meier, generally, is that Smith agreed to answer questions without a lawyer. He'd been in and out of the corrections system, Meier points out, so he knew how the process worked, and he knew that he had the to right to remain silent until a lawyer was appointed to him. And he chose not to. He answered literally hundreds of questions about his activities on March 11 without resorting to the infuriating vagueness of most guilty suspects. In many cases he offered even more information than the question demanded. Roy Smith, in fact, confirmed virtually every detail about his work at the Goldbergs' that the police asked him; the only point that they disagreed over was whether Bessie Goldberg was alive when he left.

"It isn't often that you see someone talking in that kind of detail and have it be lies," says Meier. "Because arguably the only thing he lied about—if you believe the verdict—is whether or not he killed her. Everything else he says, as far as I can tell, is a hundred percent accurate. He says he was there, he says she got a phone call, he says exactly what she was doing, cleaning the pictures, taking them down, she gave him lunch—I mean he obviously remembers exactly what was going on, how much he was paid, down to the penny, how he went outside. If there were a lot of lies, the classic situation is when you can say to the jury, 'Everything the suspect told the cops was a lie, it didn't fit.' But he tells them everything they already know. I mean I'll be honest with you: If someone was to present these police reports to me, I'm not sure I'd even authorize the police to make an arrest."

The oddest thing that Smith did was to say that he left the house later than he really did. "Why not say, 'I was in the pharmacy at 2:30'?" Meier wonders. "Let's assume he kills her after the phone call at 2:30—why doesn't he get himself out of the house? Why not say, 'I went to the pharmacy at 2:30'? Or even why admit that he went to the pharmacy at all? The people in the pharmacy say he was there at 3:05 or 3:10. The girls have him on the street at 3:05. But he seems to think it's even later, quarter to four. He's erring against himself. If he wants to cover his tracks, he wants to get out of the house as quick as he can after killing her. And here's a man who, stupid as he may be or uneducated, he knows the employment office has a record of him. They said, 'You're going to Scott Road in Belmont.' He was assigned to that house, he was married to that house. Which is why it doesn't make any sense. Why would he kill that woman? Why not go to a strange house? Why not go to the house next door? It presupposes that he killed her in an act of momentary rage, and if that's his pattern or lifestyle, one would think he would have had other incidents. The last several years I've been involved in a number of murder cases in which defendants convicted of murder were later proved to be innocent. Once someone gets locked up—even now, never mind in 1963— once Roy Smith got arrested for killing Bessie Goldberg, everyone who *thought* they saw something is now *convinced* they saw something. Every one who *thought* they may have seen a black man in the neighborhood moving quickly now *knew* they saw a black man in the neighborhood, running. That's just a human tendency."

In Meier's opinion, there was almost no doubt that Smith was innocent.

ON MARCH 6, 1976—nearly one year after Smith was supposed to have been released from Norfolk—the Advisory Board of

Pardons once again met to discuss his case. By unanimous vote they again decided to grant him his freedom, but only if the Massachusetts Executive Council concurred; by law there can be no commutation without the approval of the executive council. The date of his parole would be twelve months after the executive council made their decision, whenever that might be. The advisory board sent a letter to Governor Dukakis stating their recommendations, and on March 12, the governor signed a letter to the Executive Council saying that he concurred and would leave the final decision to them.

Smith's commutation languished at the executive council for the next four months. On July 1 Smith wrote a letter to Joan Stevens updating her on the progress of his case. He wrote that it was graduation day for the college program that he was enrolled in, but that he wouldn't be able to attend. "For the first time in my life I been very sick for over a month," he wrote. "They sent me from Norfolk Hospital to Lemuel Shattuck Hospital, in Jamaica Plain. I still have another test to go yet, I am waiting for the doctor to come back from vacation. My commutation papers are due to go up before the Governor's Council this month some time. And again it's election year and they are afraid of the kick-back, so as usual I am good on getting caught up in the worst of everything. Well, you drive slow while you are transporting those teenage bodies (smile) and take care. As always love, your friend, Roy."

On July 28 Judge Paul Chernoff received word that Smith—who had been experiencing respiratory problems for the preceding year—had been diagnosed with tuberculosis and lung cancer and was back at Shattuck Hospital. Smith had smoked his whole life and had undoubtedly started smoking even harder once he got into prison. Chernoff fired off a letter to the governor stating that, in light of Smith's illness, the advisory board recommended that Smith's sentence be commuted immediately. Two days later, on July 30, Smith began a ten-day course of radiation that would total 2,500 rads over ten days. The course would be repeated several weeks later.

On August 4 Smith's doctor, Charles Rosenbaum, wrote a letter to the governor informing him that Smith had Stage III large-cell bronchogenic carcinoma that had spread to his lymph nodes. Rosenbaum went on to say that only one in four patients with that disease responded to treatment, and of those, only half lived longer than eighteen months. For those who also have cancer in their lymph nodes—as Smith did—there was almost no survival beyond two years. If he did not respond to treatment, Smith would probably be dead in several months.

Two weeks later Paul Chernoff of the advisory board conducted a bedside hearing at Shattuck Hospital and sent a recommendation to Governor Dukakis that Smith be released. The governor signed the commutation papers and sent them over to the executive council, which commuted Smith's sentence to thirty-five years to life, making him eligible for parole immediately. The next day Smith was formally released from custody and given permission to travel to Oxford, Mississippi, but by then he was too sick to leave the his bed. The date was August 19, 1976. That same day Beryl Cohen visited Smith at the hospital, and a special services officer named Eddie Fitzmaurice showed up to deliver Smith's commutation in person. "He was dying, and he knew *I* knew he was dying," says Fitzmaurice. "He said that he appreciated what the parole board had done for him and that he was a free man. We were both kind of embarrassed by his dying. He said, 'I'm very sick,' and I said, 'I know that.' To be frank, I didn't want to belabor the point."

Fitzmaurice placed the commutation papers by Smith's bed and left him in peace. Smith made it through the night and the following day. His body was starting to shut down, and during his moments of consciousness he must have known it. He was never going to see his son or family again, he was never going to be free on the street, he was never even going to leave the room. He made it through the night of the twentieth. He made it through the following morning. He made it through the afternoon and the evening and into the start of another night.

An hour before midnight on August 21, 1976, Roy Smith died alone in a hospital bed at Lemuel Shattuck Hospital. Beside him on a nightstand was a governor's commutation and a parcel of personal letters. Whatever had actually happened at 14 Scott Road in Belmont thirteen years earlier, everyone involved was now dead.

September 2005

THE STORY ABOUT Bessie Goldberg that I heard from my parents was that a nice old lady had been killed down the street and an innocent black man went to prison for the crime. Meanwhile—unknown to anyone—a violent psychopath named Al was working alone at our house all day and probably committed the murder. In our family this story eventually acquired the tidy symbolism of a folk tale. Roy Smith was a stand-in for everything that was unjust in the world, and Bessie Goldberg was a stand-in for everything that was decent but utterly defenseless. Albert DeSalvo, of course, was a stand-in for pure random evil.

Our family's story was so perfect that I didn't question its simplicity until I was much older. Its simplicity was rooted in the fact that the tragedy on Scott Road had brushed our family but had never really affected us. That was a piece of good luck that I eventually realized could easily have been otherwise. What if, for example, my mother hadn't gone out on the day of the murder; what if she had just stayed home with me? Would Al have gotten his terrible urge and killed my mother instead of Bessie Goldberg? Would some other journalist now be interviewing me, rather than the other way around?

One of the conceits of my profession is that it can discover the truth; it can pry open the world in all its complexity and contradiction and find out exactly what happened in a certain place on a certain day. Sometimes it can, but often the truth simply isn't knowable—not, at least, in an absolute way. As I did my research I came to understand that not only was this story far messier than the one I'd grown up with, but that I would never know for sure what had actually happened in the Goldberg house that day. Without DNA evidence Smith's guilt or innocence would always be a matter of conjecture. By extension DeSalvo's possible role in the murder would also be a matter of conjecture, and I would never know for sure how close I had come to losing my mother.

So if I was to say something meaningful in this story, I would have to do it without discovering the truth. But maybe the truth isn't even the most interesting thing about some stories, I thought; maybe the most interesting thing about some stories is all the things that *could* be true. And maybe it's in the pursuit of *those* things that you understand the world in its deepest, most profound sense.

If Roy Smith had not been working at the Goldberg residence the day she was killed, the murder would quickly have been added to the list of other Boston Stranglings. It was so similar to the previous eight killings that the police initially thought they had arrested the man responsible for all of them. They hadn't. If, for argument's sake, one excludes Smith as the murderer, then Bessie Goldberg becomes the ninth in a string of ghastly sex murders in Boston. Her killer becomes a white man, because anyone else would have stood out on Scott Road. Her killer becomes someone who somehow entered her house between 3:05, when Smith left, and 3:25, when four neighborhood children started playing kickball on the street outside. Alternatively her killer becomes someone who entered her house through the back door between 3:25 and 3:50, when Israel Goldberg came home. Her killer becomes someone skilled at killing older women, because he did it so quickly and cleanly that Bessie Goldberg's glasses didn't even fall off. Her killer becomes a man with a very specific sexual compulsion, because few robbers or murderers—in fact, not even that many rapists—rape the elderly. Her killer, ultimately, becomes someone who entered her house with the sole purpose of killing her, and who carried it out in a way that not many men, psychologically or physically, would be capable of.

That is Albert DeSalvo's description of himself. Whether or not DeSalvo was the Boston Strangler is another matter, but with Roy Smith out of the picture, the man who killed Bessie Goldberg becomes exactly the man Albert DeSalvo claimed he was. If it wasn't Albert DeSalvo, it was a man very much like him. And if it was Roy Smith, it was Smith acting way in a way that he never had before in his life. Smith was a criminal, and criminals are very aware of the ways in which they might get caught. Killing Bessie Goldberg was a virtually guaranteed way of getting caught, which meant that Smith wasn't thinking very hard about getting away with it. He was either desperate for drug money when he did it, or he was momentarily insane; the only other possibility was that he was innocent. There didn't seem to be much in between.

It was with that idea in mind that I went to Oxford, Mississippi, in April 2003 to try to find the family of Roy Smith. Smith's innocence was not an idea that I could prove—it wasn't even an idea that I necessarily *believed*—but it was an idea that was at least possible. And I wanted to try that possibility out on Smith's own flesh and blood.

———

I FOUND THE Smith family through a black minister in Oxford who had known Andy, the father. They still owned property on South Sixteenth, though the old wood-frame house that Roy had grown up in had been replaced by a single-story brick house that was kept dark and heavily air-conditioned. Two of Roy's sisters and one of his brothers was still alive, and his nephew, Coach, was now in his midthirties and married. Coach was named after one of Roy's brothers and had grown up talking to Roy on the prison phone. As a child he had lived mostly with Mollie and Andy, his grandparents, but by the time he was a teenager he was spending a lot of time on the street and getting into trouble. He started dealing drugs and then he started using drugs and he did a little time in prison, and when he got out he went straight back to the street. He was finally arrested with a handgun after he and two friends stole a woman's purse in a supermarket parking lot. The courts had had enough of Coach Smith and handed him a mandatory five-year sentence. Coach Smith, like the uncle he'd never met, was now doing hard time in a state prison.

And prison was good for him—as it had been for his uncle. He told his family not to visit him and he just did his time and thought about his life. His grandmother died while he was in prison, and he went to the funeral in shackles. He dealt drugs in prison but eventually straightened out, and if he didn't find religion, he found some personal version of it that served the same purpose. He got out after five years and married his old girlfriend and got a job in Oxford and started living his life straight. He was thirty-two years old. He had saved himself. That was when I met him.

One evening Coach and I were driving back to Oxford from Memphis, and I asked him what he would do if he had killed a white woman whose house he had just cleaned. It went without saying that Coach thought his uncle was innocent, and I'd made it clear that I thought he might be but that I wasn't at all sure. I just wanted to hear what Coach had to say about the situation. Pretend you're Roy Smith, I'd said. There's a dead lady in Belmont and the police know you were there that day. Presumably they're going to come after you. What do you do?

We were driving through the Clay Hills of central Mississippi, an empty stretch of poor pine forests and tangled bayous and eroded red earth. Lone brick houses were set back on lawns with long winding driveways and unnecessary brick gateposts that lacked both gates and walls leading up to them. The sun was setting and Coach was smoking a menthol and flicking the ashes into a paper cup. He didn't seem to have to think about the question very long. "I would leave town, but I wouldn't come back down South," he said. "They'd find me in Oxford and they'd find me in Boston. I'd have gone to all my women and asked 'em for money, and if I couldn't have gotten it through the women, I'd would've robbed, stole, or whatever and got that money and got outta town. If I'm a murderer what do I give a damn about robbin' or killin'?"

That day Coach was wearing a narrow-brim houndstooth hat and brand-new blue jeans and blazing white basketball shoes. He was happy to talk almost nonstop, but he had a way of expressing things that occasionally brought me up short. His young step-daughter was one of the top students in her class, and he'd once told me that the only thing the Ku Klux Klan could never defeat was a black girl who got straight As.

"Roy was a criminal," Coach went on. "If he had to come to his feet to commit a murder he had to come to his feet to get away. Because if he did commit the crime—bein' a criminal myself—he wouldn't have been out joyriding with his friends and gettin' drunk, because that's slippin'. If you just committed a murder, what you want to do is settle down, you going to find some alibis, you going to try to do things where you wouldn't be seen. Just sit and wait till things cool off a bit. You might run into the police—what if they pick you up for public drunk? Why go out with that? If he'd committed that crime he wouldn't have been out drunk, that's the *last* thing he would do. If you commit murder, that's just like lyin'—you tell one lie you got to continue telling lies. If you commit a crime, then you got to prepare yourself for the next crime, and the next crime. And goin' out and gettin' drunk is not preparing yourself for crimes. You're in a town. Where are your friends? Who you got in Boston? You got nobody? So you go blow all your money?"

Roy was a different person than Coach, and he certainly had a drinking problem that Coach didn't. Still, the logic of the criminal mind was hard to argue with. I asked Coach what he would think if he *hadn't* killed the white lady—if he'd just cleaned her house that day—and then had read in the paper later that she'd been murdered. "If he knew this lady from Belmont was dead he was stressed out," Coach said. "He was just havin' a good time and hopin' that didn't no drama come back behind all that. It was all about hope. That was all Roy was doin'. He was hopin'."

A few months later Coach flew to Boston to meet Dorothy Hunt, who was the only one of Roy's friends I'd been able to find. By the time I'd started looking, most of the people Smith had gone drinking with that night were dead. Coach and I spent about an hour talking with Dorothy Hunt in her living room, and then we went out to dinner around the corner from where Smith was arrested. It was a miserable October night with a hard rain that soaked us as soon as we stepped out of the car. Coach was the only black man in the restaurant, and he was surprised that the two of us could walk in and take a seat without drawing any stares. After dinner we ran back to the car, and I offered to drive Coach around his uncle's old neighborhood. Back in Roy's day the neighborhood was mostly black, and Coach had expected something that looked a little more threatening.

"This isn't a bad neighborhood," Coach said as we drove down River Street. "I mean, I don't even see nobody standin' around."

I said that maybe no one was standing around because it was midnight and pouring rain.

"A little rain never stopped no standin' around," he informed me. "I guarantee you, Sebastian, *some*where in Boston, *some*body is standin' around."

COACH'S DEFINITION OF a ghetto was good—as good as any I'd ever heard from an economist. Jesse Jackson once described walking through a dangerous neighborhood and whirling around in fear when he heard footsteps behind him. It was a white man, though, not a young black man, and Jackson said that his sense of relief was one of the most painful things in his life.

If Jesse Jackson is capable of thinking that way about young black men, policemen obviously are as well, and that goes to the heart of the Roy Smith case. The entire thing—from his arrest to his interrogation to his conviction—reeked of the presumption of guilt, and nothing would be easier for me than to put him at the center of that process and watch it grind him up. But the more I found out about Smith's life, the more ambiguous he became until I actually started to resent him for disappointing me. Smith was exactly the sort of shady character that Coach had been looking for on River Street that night. At every juncture Smith made the wrong choice: He stole instead of worked, drank instead of providing for his girlfriend and child, moved from apartment to apartment instead of settling down and leading a productive life. He was a hard guy to like. The assault that he was accused of in New York was particularly troubling. How could he—a man who claimed to be innocent of murdering Bessie Goldberg—point a pistol at the head of a woman in a shoe store and pull the trigger?

The answer, of course, is that the crime report may well have been grossly distorted. The case relied exclusively on witness identification, the forensic tests on the gun were added to the report in longhand, and Smith's criminal file in Boston stated that the gun was actually made of wood. But either way Smith had made it easy for them. Smith was a criminal: he thought in criminal ways, he devised criminal solutions for ordinary problems, he went straight to the very criminal role that any racist cop or witness or juror would hope to see him in. From there it was a very short step to just assuming that he was guilty of virtually any crime he was accused of.

For this Coach cannot forgive his uncle. If Roy had been working a steady job and leading an upright life, he would never have been in Belmont in the first place. But he wasn't; he was living dollar to dollar and drink to drink and cleaning white people's houses whenever he needed money. Everything bad that happened to him followed from that. It didn't mean he killed anyone, but in Coach's eyes, his uncle still had some degree of responsibility for what happened. His uncle needed to get his shit together, and he didn't.

Still there remained the essential question, Did he do it? Did Roy Smith—in one crazed, violent moment—put his hands to Bessie Goldberg's throat, choke her, rape her, and then run out of the house with the ten and five ones that Israel Goldberg said he left

on the nightstand? Like it or not, I had developed some sort of relationship in my mind with this man, and it was important for me to
know who I was dealing with. He achieved some measure of
redemption in prison, and that was all well and good, but that is just
a footnote to the real story, which is whether I was writing about an
innocent man or a monster. It must be said that at first I thought—
I assumed—he was innocent. The story was just too familiar, too
much of an archetype for it to be otherwise. Then, as I learned more
about him, my opinion started to change. Where *did* the money he
spent on booze that night come from? Why didn't he want to go
home when he saw the cops at his apartment? And most important,
who else really could have done it?

I eventually resigned myself to the idea that I was probably writing about a man who had committed a savage, unforgivable crime.
It made me terrifically sad for Bessie Goldberg and her family, and
it made me furious at Roy. I felt deceived, in a way—deceived by
him as well as by my own assumptions. However much racism
Smith suffered as a black man in America, nothing excused that
kind of crime. It was beyond imagining; it was beyond even wanting to write about.

What changed my opinion yet again was Smith's time in prison.
It was there where he became—in my eyes—a hardworking, thoroughly decent man who refused to plea bargain and who even
refused to admit his guilt to the parole board. That was a move that
should have condemned him to prison for life. Why would someone as morally bankrupt as a rapist and murderer not fake his
remorse and get out of prison early? Why stand up for a false principle when he actually committed the murder and had the chance
to get off easy?

The state's case against Smith—which had seemed so airtight at first—also began to unravel. Forget the fact that Smith was black in a white suburb and was grilled for twelve hours by the police. Forget that his jury members were all white men who had first been screened—in their homes—by the Belmont police. (That practice was abolished after a review of Smith's case by the Massachusetts Supreme Judicial Court.) Forget that Beryl Cohen had never tried a murder case before, that he was denied access to almost all of the State's evidence, and that Smith was not only thought to be the Boston Strangler but was convicted the day after Kennedy was shot. Convicted, no less, by men from the same congressional district where Kennedy had first risen to power. Today all those factors would have been grounds for a mistrial, but they still didn't speak to Smith's actual guilt or innocence.

The state's case against Smith, however, *did* claim to speak to his actual guilt or innocence, and it has to be considered carefully. The reason this is important has nothing to do with Roy Smith or Bessie Goldberg or even Al DeSalvo; they're all dead. In some ways there is nothing less relevant than an old murder case. The reason it is important is this: Here is a group of people who have gathered to judge—and possibly execute—a fellow citizen. It's the highest calling there is, the very thing that separates us from social anarchy, and it has to be done well. A trial, however, is just a microcosm of the entire political system. When a democratic government decides to raise taxes or wage war or write child safety laws, it is essentially saying to an enormous jury, "This is our theory of how the world works, and this is our proposal for dealing with it. If our theory makes sense to you, vote for us in the next election. If it doesn't, throw us out." The ability of citizens to scrutinize the theories insisted on by their government is their only protection against abuse of power and, ultimately, against tyranny. If ordinary citizens can't coolly and rationally evaluate a prosecutor's summation in a criminal trial, they won't have a chance at calling to task a deceitful government. And *all* governments are deceitful—they're deceitful because it's easier than being honest. Most of the time, it's no more sinister than that.

Fortunately the citizenry—in Roy Smith's case, the jury—doesn't usually need much outside information to evaluate their government's theories. Erroneous arguments usually aren't even internally consistent, much less consistent with the outside world. In Smith's case the state's theory about who killed Bessie Goldberg essentially boiled down to money and time. Roy Smith arrived for work at the Goldberg residence with three dollars and twenty cents in his pocket, he was supposedly paid a little more than six dollars for his work, and he then went on to spend almost fourteen dollars that evening. The discrepancy, according to the state, was explained by the fact that Smith had stolen the money that Israel Goldberg had left on his wife's nightstand. The reason Smith killed her was so that he could get away with the theft.

Senseless murders like that happen almost every day, but in this case the theory is entirely based on information volunteered by Smith. He could have stopped the state's case in its tracks simply by telling the police he'd showed up for work not with two dollars in his pocket but with ten. Nothing could have been easier, and he would have gutted the one theory the state had for why he committed the murder. Likewise with the time issue: Prosecutor Kelley argued before the jury that too little time elapsed between Smith's departure from the house and Israel Goldberg's arrival for anyone else to have committed the murder. But one of the reasons they knew when Smith left is that he *told* them. True, investigators went on to confirm the time with other witnesses, but Smith couldn't have known that.

The cops wanted to know what time he left the Goldberg house, and he told them the truth. He told the truth despite the fact that it was sure to make him the only suspect in the murder.

Guilty murder suspects—much like governments—generally tell the truth about everything they can and then lie about the rest. They lie about the things that will get them in trouble, and successful prosecutions depend on exposing those lies to the jury. The logical problem with the state's case against Smith is that its core elements are known only because he told the truth. Admittedly the truth makes him look awfully guilty, but a theory about his guilt is incomplete without somehow taking into account the fact that he never lied about what he did that day. Not only did he not lie, he didn't change his clothes, he didn't get rid of Bessie Goldberg's address in his coat pocket, he didn't flee the area, he didn't even avoid walking past the police station in Central Square. He didn't, in other words, do any of the things that most criminals do to avoid getting caught. His most damning action was to tell Billy Cartwright to keep driving after he spotted the police waiting for him in his apartment that night. But for a black man with a criminal record to not want to talk to the police in 1963 is understandable in almost any circumstance. It certainly doesn't prove that Roy Smith committed murder.

But the problem with ruling out Smith is that there's no one to take his place; the police had no other suspects. It obviously wasn't Israel Goldberg. It wasn't any of the neighbors. It probably wasn't the mailman or the milkman or any of the people who dealt with the Goldberg household. In all likelihood it was someone passing through the neighborhood who had a history of sexual violence against women. Raping and strangling an older woman is not the sort of crime that happens in isolation from other incidents.

DeSalvo fills that description perfectly if one believes his stories about being the Boston Strangler, but many people still have their doubts. The family of Mary Sullivan, the last of the thirteen victims, was particularly skeptical of DeSalvo's claims. Decades later a television and magazine reporter named Casey Sherman, who was Mary Sullivan's nephew, had his aunt's body exhumed so that forensic experts could collect DNA evidence. (The Massachusetts attorney general's office still had semen samples from her body that had allegedly come from Albert DeSalvo but was reluctant to release them for testing.) Sherman had good reasons to doubt that DeSalvo had killed his aunt. Not only was there evidence suggesting that she had been killed late in the morning—rather than late in the afternoon, as DeSalvo had claimed—but DeSalvo also said that he had raped her. The semen found at the crime scene, however, was collected from Mary Sullivan's upper body. She had not been raped.

The exhumation was conducted in the fall of 2000 and was followed by the exhumation of DeSalvo's body one year later. Sherman described the ordeal in his heartfelt book, *A Rose for Mary*. Forensic experts hired by Sherman found no semen remaining on Mary Sullivan's upper body, though a small amount of something that had "the characteristics of semen," as Sherman put it, was found on her pubic hair. DNA extracted from that sample was compared to DNA taken from DeSalvo's body and was found *not* to match. Albert DeSalvo, Sherman concluded, had not raped his aunt and therefore had not killed her. It's not clear how much this proves, however. Because Mary Sullivan wasn't raped by *anyone*, flecks of semen in her pubic hair would have nothing to do with DeSalvo anyway. The comparison that should have been done was between DeSalvo's DNA and the semen found on her upper body. Errors in his confessions certainly cast doubt on whether he was the killer, but the DNA tests conducted by Sherman failed to prove that he was *not*.

But there remained one last crucial question. With or without the murders, DeSalvo—as a confirmed multiple rapist—had the psychological profile of someone who could have murdered Bessie Goldberg. And he was alone at my parents' house all afternoon, which put him roughly in the same neighborhood at the time of the murder. There was enough time for him—for anyone—to have slipped into the house and committed the murder between 3:05 and 3:50. It's all possible. But if DeSalvo killed Bessie Goldberg, *why didn't he say so?*

This could be why: If we assume for a moment that DeSalvo killed not only Bessie Goldberg but all the other women as well, he would have had a serious dilemma on his hands. Confessing to thirteen murders that no one else has been convicted of is easy, in a sense; the police get to clear their files, the press gets to run a sensational story, and the attorney general is probably running for higher office and gets to take credit. But there is tremendous reluctance on the part of the police to cast doubt on murders that have already been "solved." Not only does it undermine all their hard work, but everyone involved—from the cops to the jury to the prosecutor to the judge—looks like a fool. The reason it is so hard to reopen old murder cases, ultimately, is that there's nothing in it for anyone but the guy in jail.

DeSalvo would have known this. Desalvo was a man who had been in and out of the system his whole life and who had spent years in prison with other criminals. He was trying to convince the attorney general's office that he was the real Boston Strangler, and claiming a murder that had already been solved by that same office could have jeopardized everything he was trying to do. And according to Steve Delaney, there was one other issue that complicated matters. There was essentially a race war going on at Walpole at the time, and a white inmate who helped a black inmate get out of prison would immediately have been seen as a traitor. Whites and blacks stuck to their own groups for safety, and any inmate who was cast out would have had no protection whatsoever. Whatever DeSalvo's personal views on race were, his security in prison depended on the fact that he was firmly embedded in the white power structure. Helping Smith would have alienated the very people DeSalvo needed most.

When I was in Mississippi with Coach Smith, I asked him to put himself in his uncle's shoes and tell me what he would do. Would he flee? Would he hide? Would he continue as if nothing had happened? Coach's answers didn't prove anything, but they did shed some light on the workings of the criminal mind. And one can pose those same kinds of questions about DeSalvo. There is some chance that DeSalvo never killed anyone; that is just a reality that can't be ignored. But there is also some chance that he did. And suppose it was true: Suppose he really was the Boston Strangler; suppose he really did kill Bessie Goldberg. What would his relationship with Roy Smith have been like? Here would be a man, after all, who was serving time for a crime that DeSalvo had committed. Smith was DeSalvo's twin, in a way—his unwitting soul-mate—and everything that happened to him in the judicial system really should have happened to DeSalvo.

So if you were DeSalvo, what would *you* do? Would you, for example, study newspaper photos of the Goldberg house well enough to know what kind of gutters they had? Would you follow Smith's fate in prison closely enough to know which questions he failed on his lie detector test? Would you remember when the ten-year anniversary of his conviction rolled around?

And if you didn't remember the date, others might. It was the evening of November 25, 1973, and apparently there was someone out there on the cell blocks who wanted to kill you. Not just kill you; wanted to stab you over and over again until your chest was in shreds. DeSalvo had a lot of troubles in prison, and there is no way to know which one he was worried about that night. But if you were he—if you were in a prison cleaved by racial violence and a black man was doing time for your crime, a black man whose life you knew about in the greatest detail, and the ten-year anniversary of his life sentence came up—if all these things were true, would you fake a stomach ailment to get into the hospital for a few days?

Well?

Is that conceivably something you might do?

Further Reading

Like most works of journalism, this book relies heavily on the research of others. I would like to call attention to a few books that were particularly helpful to me. For an account of life at Parchman Farm, I consulted *Down on Parchman Farm*, by William Banks Taylor (Columbus: Ohio State University Press, 1999), and *Worse than Slavery: Parchman Farm and the Ordeal of Jim Crow Justice*, by David M. Oshinsky (New York: Simon & Schuster, 1996). For a general account of racism and lynching in America, nothing beats Philip Dray's superb *At the Hands of Persons Unknown* (New York: Modern Library, 2002). An interesting counterpart to that is Don H. Doyle's *Faulkner's County: The Historical Roots of Yoknapatawpha* (Chapel Hill: University of North Carolina Press, 2001). Also helpful is *Faulkner's World* (Oxford: University Press of Mississippi, 1997), which shows life in Oxford, Mississippi, in the 1950s and 1960s through the lens of photographer Martin Dain.

For a more contemporary look at racism and the civil rights movement, *Reporting Civil Rights* (New York: Library of America,

2003) compiles press reports from 1963 to 1973. *We Charge Genocide* (New York: International Publishers, 1970), edited by William Patterson, is an important—though out-of-print—documentation of racial injustice. And, *Race, Crime and the Law*, by Randall Kennedy (New York: Vintage, 1998), offers a devastating critique of racial inequities in the legal system.

A lively account of the history of Central Square can be found in *Crossroads: Stories of Central Square, Cambridge, Massachusetts 1912–2000*, by Sarah Boyer (Cambridge: Cambridge Historical Commission, 2001). The book has great archival photographs of Cambridge during the past century. Other archival photographs of Chelsea, Massachusetts, can be found in Margaret Harriman Clarke's *Images of America: Chelsea* (Charleston, SC: Arcadia Publishing, 1998). For a history of Jewish emigration to America, I consulted *Jews, God and History*, by Max I. Dimont (New York: New American Library, 1962).

There are many excellent books on criminal investigation, but I relied most heavily on *Practical Homicide Investigation: Tactics, Procedures, and Forensic Techniques*, by Vernon J. Geberth, and *Forensic Pathology*, by Dominick J. Di Maio and Vincent J. M. Di Maio. (Both books are published by CRC Press in New York, in 1996 and 1989, respectively. I should mention that the crime-scene photographs in these books are so disturbing that I required months to get them out of my head.) A full account of the case of Larry Swartz, who murdered his parents in Annapolis, Maryland, in 1984, can be found in *Sudden Fury: A True Story of Adoption and Murder*, by Leslie Walker (New York: St. Martin's Press, 1989).

The two classic books on Albert DeSalvo are *The Boston Strangler*, by Gerold Frank (New York: New American Library, 1996), and *Confessions of the Boston Strangler*, by George Rae (New York:

Pyramid Books, 1967). Two other well-known books on the topic are *The Boston Stranglers*, by Susan Kelly (New York: Birch Lane Press, 1995), and *A Rose for Mary: The Hunt for the Real Boston Strangler*, by Casey Sherman (Boston: Northeastern University Press, 2003). Both Kelly and Sherman contend that DeSalvo was not the killer he claimed to be, and no serious study of the topic can be made without carefully considering what these two authors have to say.

Finally I consulted more law books than I care to remember or can bring myself to list; suffice it to say that any introductory textbook on criminal law will give one the basics. Beyond that, you're on your own.

ACKNOWLEDGMENTS

First and foremost I would like to thank my wife, Daniela, for her endless and indispensable advice while I was writing this book. She is in many ways the wisest reader I know. I also thank many friends—particularly John Falk, Rob Leaver, Alan Huffman, Teun Voeten, and Scott Anderson—for reading and commenting on my work as it progressed. My mother, Ellen, and my father, Miguel, have also read and reread this work many times, for which I am deeply appreciative. On the professional end of things I would like to thank my agent, Stuart Krichevsky; his assistants, Shana Cohen and Elizabeth Coen; my editors, Starling Lawrence and Morgen Van Vorst; my copyeditors, Janet Byrne and Sue Llewellyn; my in-house publicists, Louise Brockett and Elizabeth Riley; and my personal publicist, Cathy Saypol, for their advice and great work in seeing this book to completion. I am also very indebted to Austin Merrill and Sady Cohen for their exhaustive research and fact-checking. A wonderful woman named Mary Dunn, who helped me in the early stages of my research, tragically passed away before the book was completed. She is greatly missed.

This book incorporates, in one form or another, the knowledge of many people who gave so generously of their time. I was given incredible legal advice—in one case, it virtually amounted to a private tutorial—by Judge Chris Muse, Judge Paul Chernoff, Judge Robert Bohn, David Meier (prosecutor), Karolyn Tontarski (medical examiner), Dr. Alison Fife (forensic psychiatrist), Randy Chapman (attorney), and Brownlow Speer (appellate lawyer). Steve Delaney devoted an enormous amount of time and effort, and I cannot thank him enough. In Mississippi I was greatly aided—not to mention fed, entertained, and sheltered—by Richard and Lisa Howorth and their wonderful family. Many thanks to them. Coach Smith appears as a character in this book, of course, but he is now also a good friend. His utter honesty about himself and the world he comes from was truly inspiring.

Finally I would like to recognize the numerous people who agreed to be interviewed for this book. I will not list them individually because their names appear in the text, but I would like to say that I do realize how painful some of those interviews must have been. This book is about a murder and the lives that were damaged in its wake, and there is no way to have a pleasant conversation about something like that. I am very, very appreciative that the people involved had the courage to speak with me.